1977 Supplement to the American Civil Liberties Union Policy Guide

1977 Supplement to the American Civil Liberties Union Policy Guide

Lexington Books
D.C. Heath and Company
Lexington, Massachusetts
Toronto

Members of the American Civil Liberties Union may order copies of the
1976 Policy Guide of the American Civil Liberties Union from the ACLU,
22 East 40th Street, New York, New York 10016.

Nonmembers of the ACLU may order copies of the *1976 Policy Guide of
the American Civil Liberties Union* from Lexington Books, D.C. Heath and
Company, 125 Spring Street, Lexington, Massachusetts 02173.

Library of Congress Cataloging in Publication Data

American Civil Liberties Union.
  1977 supplement to the American Civil Liberties Union policy guide.

  Includes indexes.
  1. Civil rights—United States. 2. American Civil Liberties Union.
I. American Civil Liberties Union. 1976 policy guide of the American Civil
Liberties Union. II. Title.
KF4749.A74 Suppl.   342'.73'085   78-19573
ISBN 0-669-02624-7

Published simultaneously in Canada.

Printed in the United States of America.

International Standard Book Number: 0-669-02624-7

Library of Congress Catalog Card Number: 78-19573

TABLE OF CONTENTS

*Policies marked with a single asterisk (*) represent new paragraphs to existing policies.

v

**Policies marked with a double asterisk (**) represent new policy adopted by the ACLU Board of Directors since the publication of the 1976 Policy Guide.

xi

***This policy combines the original statement on Use of Prior Sexual History in Rape Trials which appeared in the 1976 Policy Guide (see policy #229) and the recent additions on sexual assault adopted by the Board of Directors, under the new policy titled Sexual Assault Laws.

****The Board of Directors undertook a comprehensive review of the policies in the Immigration and Naturalization and Aliens sections of the 1976 Policy Guide. The policy changes adopted represent additions, deletions, and necessary editorial contractions of the old policies, #322 through #330. Since the policy changes are quite extensive and do not exactly track the 1976 Guide pages, we have omitted the 1976 Guide page number for some of the policies in this section.

INTRODUCTION

This book is the first supplement to the revised *1976 Policy Guide of the American Civil Liberties Union*. It contains all the substantive and organizational policies adopted by the Board of Directors over a 21-month period, from April 1976 through December 1977.[1]

This *Supplement* is being distributed to those persons who possess the 1976 revised guide. If the reader does not have the 1976 revised guide, it is important that he/she not take the *Supplement* as *the* guide. Please contact the national ACLU for the 1976 revision. In sum, the *Supplement* is not a replacement for the 1976 *Guide*, but should be examined against the original text to determine the full scope of the policy area covered. We are not repeating here the detailed explanation of why the *Policy Guide* was established, what represents policy, how policy is made and how the *Guide* should be used. These matters are fully discussed in the introduction to the 1976 revised edition.

The policies in this *Supplement* cover four distinct areas: 1) totally new policies; 2) additions to, or substitutions for, existing policies; 3) policies with minor editorial changes; and 4) policies from the 1976 *Guide* that had never been formally approved by the Board but represented positions taken in legal briefs, press releases, and committee reports. Under a new review procedure, the Board has now given final approval.

The *Supplement* continues an experiment begun in 1976 by adding to (or updating) many full policy texts a section labeled Further Information (not policy). This covers background information on key Supreme Court decisions and national legislation. Such amplification places the policy in a broader context but should not be confused with the policy itself. It is important to note that the court decisions summarized may not be the latest Supreme Court view of the issue. The reader is urged to check with legal publications, such as *U.S. Law Week*, to learn about more recent Supreme Court actions.

Although the *Supplement* is a companion to the 1976 revised *Guide*, to facilitate use of both books the table of contents in the *Supplement* contains a combined listing of all ACLU policies adopted through December 1977. The reader may, in some cases, be confused by seeing the same policy numbers in the 1976 edition and the *Supplement*. We have not renumbered the 1976 policies to fit the *Supplement* numbers, a step which will be taken when a totally new policy guide is prepared in the future. The table of contents in the *Supplement* should be used only for the 1976-1977 policies in the *Supplement*. The contents page is divided into three columns: the first shows the policy number and title, the second indicates where the policy can be found in the 1976 *Guide*, and the third notes the page in the *Supplement* where the new policy can be found.

---

[1] One exception to this time period is the March 1978 policy on sentencing. It is included because the 1977 policy on this subject was a provisional policy and we wanted to show the Board's final action.

There are two indexes to the *Supplement*. The first deals with material found in the Further Information (not policy) sections connected to the policies; the second is the reference to the policy texts. As in the table of contents, there is a duplication of numbers between the *Supplement* and the *Guide*. Use the index in the *Supplement* for policies in the *Supplement* only.

***

Special mention should be made of my colleague, Barbara Eichman, the ACLU's Librarian-Archivist, who helped in more ways than can be described in the preparation of the *Supplement*. Her assistance in the editorial preparation deserves particular tribute.

Summer 1978

Alan Reitman
Associate Executive Director

FREEDOM OF BELIEF, EXPRESSION, AND ASSOCIATION

Censorship

Policy #1

Prior Restraint and Official Censorship

(a) Believing that pre-censorship is the most dangerous of all curtailments of the freedom of expression guaranteed by the First Amendment, the ACLU opposes any governmental restriction or punishment, prior to publication or exhibition, of any form of expression on grounds of obscenity. [Board Minutes, April 16, 1962 and February 14-15, 1970.]

In particular, the Union believes that municipal or state censorship boards which screen and license motion pictures prior to public exhibition engage in unconstitutional pre-censorship of expression. Though the Supreme Court upheld the constitutionality of such prior restraints by a narrow majority in *Times Film Corp. v. Chicago* (1961), in *Freedman v. Maryland* (1965), the Court weakened government control of content by setting forth constitutionally mandated procedural requirements "to obviate the dangers of a censorship system." The Supreme Court has declared that expression of ideas through motion pictures falls within the free speech and press guarantees of the First and Fourteenth Amendments (*Burstyn v. Wilson* 1952). Pre-censorship of motion pictures is unconstitutional because it inhibits the full and free exchange of views through a constitutionally protected means of communication. It is dangerous because it surrenders to the secret deliberations of a government agency a determination of the "public good" which is properly the decision of the entire community. The function of the censor, after all, is to suppress. Further, the nature of the office subjects it to pressures from those who have created it—those who believe there are subjects which ought not to be presented to the public. [Board Minutes, June 18-19, 1977.]

(See also policy on Private Pressure Groups and on Access to Government Information.)

***

(b) The Union opposes any law and ordinance that establishes police censorship of books or gives arbitrary powers to license commissioners to control the character of literature sold on newsstands or the subject matter of plays. It is in fact opposed to any official determination that deprives any form of expression of the protection of the First Amendment, but if such a case is brought into a court of law the issue will at least be decided by judicially acceptable criteria, and the court's decision will be subject to some review. This

3

cannot be said for official censorship by state and county commissions and local review boards that select and ban "objectionable" books and magazines, often at the behest of strong, special interest pressure groups. [Board Minutes, January 19, 1931, January 26, 1931, April 29, 1946; Minutes of National Council on Freedom from Censorship, April 1, 1953; *Freedom from Censorship*, 1949; Weekly Bulletin, February 4, 1963.]

***

(c) The right of newspapers and radio-TV stations to carry news of gambling events (horse races, for example) in states where these activities are legal is supported by the ACLU. Federal legislation restricting dissemination of gambling information is permissible only if it preserves this right. Prohibition of such communication, where criminal intent is absent, is unconstitutional censorship by prior restraint. [Board Minutes, June 26, 1960; Minutes of Free Speech Committee, January 28, 1952, March 4, 1955.]

***

(d) No government agency may act as a censor by screening publications for sale on newsstands in government buildings or military bases, or in any way suggest "official" approval or disapproval of any publication sold on government property. If a government agency undertakes to provide facilities for the distribution of publications, it must conform to the principles that protect the free press. It is likewise improper for a government employee or any private person to use government property as a means of displaying or disseminating purely personal views, thus lending to those views an aura of "official" sanction. [Minutes of Censorship Committee, February 25, 1964; News Releases, September 4, 1959, April 24, 1962, May 3, 1962, September 2, 1963, May 25, 1964.]

***

Further Information (not policy)

After upholding pre-censorship of motion pictures in 1961, the Court offset this decision when it later ruled that such a process avoids the test of unconstitutionality only if it complies with procedural safeguards mandated by the First Amendment. In *Freedman v. Maryland* (1965), the Maryland motion picture censorship statute was held to violate the First Amendment guarantee of freedom of expression because it lacked "sufficient safeguards for confining the censor's action to judicially determined constitutional limits . . . " The following procedural safeguards were required in *Freedman*: 1) the burden of proving that the film is unprotected expression must rest on the censor; 2) while the state may require advance submission of all films, a proper sensitivity to freedom of expression is assured by the requirement that only a judicial determination in an adversary proceeding can uphold a valid final restraint; 3) the exhibitor must be assured that the censor will, within a specified brief period, either issue, license, or commence judicial proceedings; 4) any restraint imposed in advance of a final judicial determination must be limited to the shortest fixed period compatible with sound judicial resolution and 5) the procedure must assure a prompt final judicial decision.

In light of the *Freedman* decision, the Court has overturned several state statutes which provided for official censorship where provisions of the statute were not narrowly drawn and lacked definite standards and adequate procedural safeguards. These cases were *Interstate Circuit Inc. v. Dallas* (1968) and *Teitel Film Corp. v. Cusak* (1968).

Only the state of Maryland and several municipalities, including Chicago and Dallas, continue to have active licensing requirements for films. Maryland's statutory system was found to be consistent with the Supreme Court's present criteria in *Waggonheim v. Maryland State Board of Censors* (1969), and affirmed in *Grove Press v. Maryland State Board of Censors* (1970). Those criteria require the following three safeguards for First Amendment rights in a system of movie censorship: (a) the censor must have the burden of instituting court proceedings; (b) any pre-judicial restraint can only be imposed briefly and to preserve the status quo; and (c) there must be a prompt judicial determination of obscenity.

In the related field of the musical theater, the Supreme Court applied the *Freedman* standards to invalidate a prior restraint. In *Southeastern Promotions Ltd. v. Conrad* (1975), the promoters of the rock musical "Hair" challenged a refusal by the local municipal board to permit its presentation on the ground that the production would not be "in the best interest of the community." Noting that municipal theaters are "public forums designed for and dedicated to expressive activities," the Supreme Court held that the municipal board's refusal constituted a prior restraint imposed without affording the procedural safeguards required by *Freedman v. Maryland*.

Policy #2

Mail Censorship

(a) The post is protected by the First Amendment. To censor mail is to censor speech—the exchange of ideas between people. It is a prior restraint in violation of the First Amendment for the Post Office to bar from the mails, seize, or impound, even temporarily, publications or private communications alleged by Post Office officials to be obscene or seditious. Although the ACLU is opposed to all laws that restrain freedom of communication and expression, it is particularly concerned to ensure that no communication will be subject to restraint *before* it enters into public circulation. [Board Minutes, July 25, 1949; Minutes of Free Speech Committee, June 9, 1953, March 16, 1954; Testimony before Senate Committee on the Post Office and Civil Service, August 21, 1962.]

It is similarly unconstitutional for the Customs Bureau to seize or exclude materials on the grounds of sedition or obscenity prior to the dissemination of such materials. [Board Minutes, June 15, 1953.]

For these reasons the ACLU also opposes legislation that would bar racial or religious "hate" literature from the mails. [Board Minutes, January 31, 1944, February 14, 1944.] (See also policy on Libel.]

The Union is opposed to federal legislation which declares that obscene material is non-mailable and imposes criminal penalties for use of the mail to transmit material adjudged to be obscene.

Two laws have been passed especially to curb the mailing of obscene materials. One permits any person to notify the Postmaster General of a personal wish not to receive any sexually oriented advertisements through the mails and prohibits the mailing of sexually oriented advertisements to anyone whose name is on the Postmaster's list of such persons. A second requires the labeling of sexually oriented mail which would hold the Post Office responsible for not delivering mail so labeled to any person who has indicated through designated channels a desire not to receive it.

When this legislation was before the Congress the ACLU opposed it, noting three principal objections: 1) they would prohibit material that is not obscene by any standard ever accepted by the Supreme Court, even for minors; 2) they would sharply limit the distribution of sexually oriented material to adults as well as to minors; and 3) the requirement for the marking of sexually oriented mail would reduce the individual's right to choose freely and without constraint what the person wishes to read. The effect of marking sexually oriented material would be very similar to that of the statute which required individuals receiving mail from Communist countries to go through special procedures in order to claim it. Particularly in a small community, the addressee of marked mail might feel constrained not to accept it for fear of social disapproval; thus, the theory of free choice would not hold up in practice.

The ACLU maintains that the burden of preventing the exposure of children to offensive or pornographic material ultimately rests with parents. The Union holds that censorship instituted to protect children inevitably affects the freedom of adults to read and view what they please. [Board Minutes, June 18-19, 1977; Testimony Before Subcommittee No. 3 of House Committee on the Judiciary, December 10, 1969.] (See also policy on Obscenity and Censorship.)

***

(b) The Union opposes the establishment of a fee for a Post Office grant of second-class mailing privileges because of its harmful effect solely on small publications expressing minority opinions. [Board Minutes, March 21, 1932.]
POLICY UNDER REVIEW.

***

Further Information (not policy)

The Supreme Court has upheld federal criminal convictions for use of the mails to carry obscene material. *Hamling v. United States* (1974) is the key Supreme Court case, which involved a federal conviction for mailing an advertisement for the defendants' illustrated edition of the Report of the

President's Commission on Obscenity and Pornography. The jury was unable to reach a verdict on the obscenity of the Report itself, but found the advertisements obscene. (See policy on Obscenity and Censorship concerning unconstitutionality of the Supreme Court's efforts to define "obscenity".)

An earlier Supreme Court decision, *Blount v. Rizzi* (1971), invalidated a federal postal "mail-block" statute which had allowed return to the sender of any obscene matter on the ground that the statute failed to comply with the safeguard mandated in the movie prior censorship cases. (See policy on Obscenity and Censorship.)

The Postal Reorganization Act of 1970 (1) allows the Postal Service to refuse to deliver materials to an individual who has informed the Service that he or she does not wish to receive such materials, considered by that person "in his sole discretion ... to be erotically arousing or sexually provocative," and (2) requires mailers of "sexually-oriented advertisements" to purchase from the Post Office lists of persons who have indicated that they don't wish to receive such advertisements, and to remove those names from their mailing lists. The first of these provisions was upheld by the Supreme Court in *Rowan v. Post Office Department* (1970) in which the Court rejected contentions that First Amendment rights were violated. The second has been upheld by a Federal District Court in *Pent-R-Books v. U.S. Postal Service* (1971). On the other hand, a Federal District Court has invalidated substantial portions of a companion provision authorizing judicial enforcement through various forms of civil injunctive relief on the ground that they impermissibly infringed on the mailer's right to communicate to willing recipients, *U.S. v. Treatman* (1976).

There is currently no federal legislation specifically prohibiting the mailing to a minor of any matter "harmful to minors." A provision in the pending criminal code legislation (S.1437) would make it a federal offense to disseminate obscene material to a minor, although obscenity is defined pursuant to the standards for adults as defined by the Supreme Court in *Miller v. California.*

Although the Supreme Court has held that possession of obscene materials within the privacy of one's home cannot be made a crime without unconstitutional infringement of the First Amendment, *Stanley v. Georgia* (1969), the Court has refused to apply *Stanley* to invalidate the federal mail obscenity statute as it applies to the distribution of obscene materials to willing adult recipients. It was split inconclusively on the constitutionality of the federal statute forbidding the importation of obscenity for private use. *United States v. 37 Photographs* (1971).

Policy #3

Private Pressure Groups

The right of protest is an essential element of the First Amendment's guarantee of freedom of expression. Whether such protest be exercised by an individual or a group it deserves legal protection as a valid demonstration of free speech and as a useful means of increasing the diversity of information and opinion available to the public.

In recent times, different groups of citizens have banded together to publicize their opposition, on various grounds, to particular films, books, magazines, radio or TV programs, or other organs of communication. These protests have taken different forms. There can clearly be no question about supporting those forms of peaceful protest, such as public speeches and meetings which follow traditional civil liberties paths.

However, difficult questions arise for civil libertarians when certain other forms of protest, such as picketing or organized boycotting, are utilized. Frequently such actions are regarded as necessary to achieve access to media outlets, or even to influence the decision of those responsible for deciding what material a medium of communication will present. Actions of the latter type, while conveying an idea, may also be seen as a tactic whose purpose is not only to protest but to punish those who disseminate the opposed material.

Even where the consequence of such tactics is to curb expression of opinion, such activity is nevertheless not inconsistent with the guarantees of the First Amendment. However, while recognizing that all methods of communication convey information and opinion, the ACLU is concerned that such organized group activity can result in the removal of material to which members of the public may wish access.

Therefore, although such activity may be legally permissible, the ACLU believes that in situations where the result or the likely future consequence of such activity will be to remove material or to close down a media outlet, the ACLU may call attention to these consequences, and urge media officials to respect the principle of public access to all materials.

The likely consequence of coercive pressure group activity should be determined by the Union through an examination of the facts of particular cases as they arise. In making its determination, ACLU will examine such criteria as the exact methods employed by the pressure group, the number of available outlets in the affected community and all other criteria which ACLU deems relevant in the particular instance. At no time during its consideration will the Union focus on the content of the given material involved or make any distinction with regard to different types of media in determining whether or not to oppose a particular example of pressure group activity. [Board Minutes, June 18-19, 1977.]

(See also policy on Selection of School and Library Materials and Pressure Group Attacks.)

Obscenity and Censorship

(a) The ACLU opposes any restraint, under obscenity statutes, on the right to create, publish or distribute materials to adults or the right of adults to choose the materials they read or view. Freedom of speech and press and freedom to read can be safeguarded effectively only if the First Amendment is applied as it was written and intended—to prohibit any restriction on these basic rights. In pursuing this policy, the ACLU emphasizes that it is neither urging the circulation nor evaluating the merit of material charged with being obscene.

***

(b) Obscenity statutes which punish the distribution of material purchased or view by minors violate the First Amendment, and inevitably restrict the right to publish and to distribute such materials to adults. The complex social problems which prompt such statutes cannot be solved by avoiding their real causes and making freedom of speech and press a diversionary whipping boy.

The ACLU is well aware of the concern of parents, clergy and community officials about the exposure of children to what many regard as hard-core pornography, whether through its availability at neighborhood stores and newsstands or by its unsolicited dissemination through the mails. The Supreme Court has held that the distribution of such material to minors is not protected by the First Amendment. However, the Union maintains that a causal relationship between exposure to obscenity and juvenile delinquency has never been carried to the point of definitive proof. (See policy on Comic Books.)

As a practical matter it would appear that there can be no legal substitute for parental responsibility. Whereas the avowed dealer in pornography is usually astute enough to keep minors out of the emporium, the proprietor of a small candy store cannot effectively censor the hundreds of paperback books displayed on racks. While a proprietor might decline to display a periodical with a patently offensive cover—and might well be persuaded to do so at the request of customers—it is unrealistic to expect an examination of the contents of every publication offered for sale. Coercive sanctions would inevitably threaten the distribution of non-pornographic materials.

***

(c) The ACLU believes that the constitutional guarantees of free speech and press apply to all expression and that all limitations of expression on the ground of obscenity are unconstitutional. But so long as courts sustain such limitations in any form, it will also work to minimize their restrictive effect. Under the First Amendment and the due process clause of the Fifth Amendment, such statutes should be required to define precisely the forms of proscribed speech, provide strict procedural safeguards, and choose the least restrictive methods of regulation.

The following safeguards for freedom of expression should be required:

1) The statutory definition of obscenity must be drawn precisely and narrowly limited to the category of materials which the Supreme Court has determined to be "obscene."

2) Book publishers and bookstores, motion picture producers, exhibitors and play producers and actors and others involved in theatrical productions, and libraries and museums, should not be threatened with the sanctions of criminal statutes for distributing or being connected with a work before it has been determined obscene in an adversary civil proceeding. The state should be required to select a civil proceeding, as the least restrictive method of censorship.

3) Obscenity statutes should be required to provide for prompt trial, determination and appellate review within specified time periods; and to require proof of scienter, under clearly defined and reasonable standards.

4) Obscenity statutes should assure defendants the right to counsel; and, if a defendant is acquitted, the defendant should be entitled to recover the costs and reasonable attorneys' fees incurred in defending the person's First Amendment rights.

5) Publishers, booksellers, exhibitors, play producers and others involved in theatrical production and places where art is exhibited should not be submitted to harrassment by a multiplicity of proceedings. The state should not be entitled to subject a work to more than one civil proceeding to determine its obscenity. This could be accomplished either by requiring that its Attorney General institute such proceeding (or designate a district or county attorney to do so), or by providing that once an obscenity proceeding has been commenced in a state against a work, no other proceeding may be instituted against the same work in other counties, cities or towns until and unless there has been a final judgment that the work is obscene.

6) The bookseller or motion picture exhibitor or play producer, or museum or art gallery proprietor should not be obliged to risk punishment by misjudging the age of a minor. Such persons should not be required to keep records of evidence submitted by minors; and should be entitled to rely reasonably on a minor's statement of age (e.g., if the child is actually within three years of the age claimed to be).

7) There should not be a variable standard of obscenity for minors.

8) With reference to obscenity, no state should be entitled to define a minor as anyone over the age of sixteen.

***

(d) The ACLU has long maintained that the Supreme Court's 1957 definition of obscenity (*Roth v. United States*)—"whether to the average person, applying community standards, the dominant theme of the material taken as a whole appeals to prurient interest"—is erroneous because this type of judgment is inevitably subjective and personal. Courts and juries continue to differ over what constitutes obscenity, often including in that category books that have won world-wide acclaim.

Similarly, the now-overruled standard that to be judged obscene a work must be "utterly without redeeming social value" is imprecise and uncertain. It is impossible to draw the exact line between "important" and "worthless" material because the informed, critical community is itself just as often divided on the issue of the social importance as on the "appeal to prurient interest" of any given work. Attempts to define "obscenity" frequently result in condemning most severely expression of a controversial nature—the very kind of speech for whose protection the First Amendment was written. For these reasons the Union is deeply dismayed by the trend toward the imposition of unprecedentedly heavy sentences on convictions in obscenity cases, involving complex constitutional questions of freedom of speech. [Board Minutes, April 16, 1962 and February 14-15, 1970.]

***

(e) The ACLU opposes all zoning plans restricting the availability of books, movies and other communications media because of their content. The ACLU has long opposed any restraint on the dissemination of materials on grounds of obscenity. It therefore believes that zoning plans designed to regulate so-called pornographic materials comprise another form of restraint that impinges on constitutionally protected speech. The breadth of zoning ordinances inevitably inhibits the full and free exchange of information and expression. [Board Minutes, June 18-19, 1977.]

***

(f) While the ACLU may vigorously dislike and reject sexual exploitation of children for commercial purposes, activities in publishing and disseminating printed or visual materials are wholly protected by the First Amendment. [Board Minutes, September 24-25, 1977.] (See also policy on Mail Censorship.)

***

Further Information (not policy)

Under the ACLU policy above the tri-partite test established by the Supreme Court in *Miller v. California* (1973) is similarly deficient. The elements of that test are: 1) whether the average person, applying contemporary community standards, (interpreted to mean standards of the local community) would find that the work taken as a whole appeals to the prurient interest; 2) whether the work depicts or describes, in a patently offensive way, sexual conduct specifically defined by the applicable state law; and 3) whether the work, taken as a whole, lacks serious literary, artistic, political or scientific value. Like the earlier test, this standard also involves subjective and personal judgments under criteria which are imprecise and uncertain.

The Supreme Court explained more fully the impact of the *Miller* "community standards" test in *Jenkins v. Georgia* (1974) and *Hamling v. U.S.* (1974). Juries need not be given explicit instructions as to what community is the relevant one for determining standards; the jury's understanding of a state or country-wide community is acceptable. This is true even where the conviction is under a federal statute. The effect of this is to give states considerable leeway in defining the relevant community and to allow attempts to apply the most restrictive standards possible in attempts to define obscenity.

In *McKinney v. Alabama* (1969), the Court held that the procedure by which a state ascertains whether certain materials are obscene must be one which ensures the necessary sensitivity to freedom of expression. Specifically, the Court held that a defendant in a criminal obscenity proceeding could not be foreclosed from litigating the obscenity of the material even though it had been declared obscene in a separate prior civil proceeding where he/she was not a party to that proceeding.

In *Marks v. United States* (1977), the Court held that the due process clause of the Fifth Amendment precluded retroactive application of the standards articulated in *Miller v. California* to the extent that those standards impose criminal liability for conduct not punishable under earlier standards.

Policy #7

Access to Government Information

(a) *Censorship of Unclassified Information*

Government censorship of unclassified information is an unconstitutional abridgement of free expression. The Union is deeply concerned that agencies of the government have arbitrarily suppressed news and information of public interest and thus narrowed "the marketplace of opinion." Government agencies can, of course, withhold truly secret information directly relevant to national security (see part b below), but it appears that in a great number of instances information has been withheld on matters having nothing at all to do with national security. Federal agencies can prevent, in addition, the disclosure of personnel and medical files, trade secrets, or raw data which may unjustifiably suggest criminal activity or malfeasance on the part of a public servant, and protect the details of their decision-making processes in order to allow serious intra-agency consideration of all kinds of proposals, even unpopular ones. But even these necessary safeguards must not be allowed to serve as a cloak for inefficiencies or unwise or even unproper behavior about which the public has the right to know. [Board Minutes, October 24, 1955; *A Report on the Denial to the American Press of Access to Information in the Federal Government*, by Allen Raymond, October 1955; Minutes of Free Speech Committee, December 21, 1954, October 23, 1963; Report by Samuel Hendel, 1965; News Release, March 11, 1955.]

The trend toward unwarranted secrecy within the executive branch of the federal government and in Congress itself has grown steadily since World War II under administrations of both parties. This development has already curtailed the power of the press and even of Congress to be of service to the people by finding out what goes on in government. It has been accompanied by practices of doubtful constitutionality within the executive branch—practices which are thereby concealed from the public—and has advanced to the point where the civil liberties of the people themselves are threatened and where some prudent remedial action by Congress is necessary to protect this vital area of the First Amendment, the public's right to know. [Board Minutes, October 24, 1955; Raymond Report, 1955.]

The Union opposes even the voluntary curtailment of public access to non-secret information, such as the plan proposed in the 1950's under which business groups would have voluntarily cooperated with the government to prevent unclassified but potentially valuable information from reaching enemy nations through technical journals and similar means. It is vital that the line between secret and non-secret data be clearly drawn. Unclassified material should not be restricted at all. [Board Minutes, October 15, 1951; Minutes of Free Speech Committee, December 21, 1954; News Release, March 11, 1955.]

The ACLU supports revision of the Administrative Procedure Act designed to disgorge information from public agencies unless withheld for compelling and legitimate reasons. The manner in which exemption criteria are applied in practice will bear close watching. Specifically, the Union seeks a declaration of legislative intent that all regulations and instructions to security investigators covering their practices and procedures during interviews should be made available as public records and not withheld as related solely to "internal" personnel rules and practices. [Board Minutes, February 14, 1966.]

***

(b) *Secrecy of Information on Grounds of National Defense and Foreign Policy*

The achievement of government of and by the people requires that the people know what the government is doing. The right to know is a necessary corollary to the right of expression guaranteed by the First Amendment. In political matters, the right of expression is meaningless without the right to know. While the conduct of an effective national defense and foreign policy may justify the withholding of certain information for a limited period, no information should remain undisclosed or be classified except for compelling reasons, in situations such as set forth below. The burden of justifying any non-disclosure or classification shall always remain with the government.

The need and right of the people to know outweighs any governmental interest in concealing military action the government is taking or sponsoring, the presence of United States military or para-military forces in foreign countries, the provision of United States military or economic assistance to foreign countries or insurgent movements, and any decisions or diplomatic commitments the United States has made to do any of the foregoing.[1] The government has a positive duty to disclose information in these categories contemporaneously with the events and without waiting for a particular request.

This duty of contemporaneous disclosure does not require that the government disclose to the public:[2]

1) technical details of military operations or weaponry, knowledge of which would be of benefit to another nation;

2) the conduct or product of the gathering of foreign intelligence by technical means (satellites, submarines, lasers)[3], so long as the types of techniques employed are made public.

3) military contingency plans in respect of foreign powers, but not including plans or surveillance in respect of domestic activity.[4]

Information that has been withheld in the interest of national defense or foreign policy and that the government is not under a duty to disclose contemporaneously shall be made available as soon as the need for its withholding is past, and no later than a short fixed period after origination. Short extensions of this period should be available only for compelling reasons and on the personal certification of the President or the head of a Department.

Information that the government may not withhold may not be protected by administrative, criminal, or other judicial sanctions.[5]

Judicial review shall be available to any citizen to compel the provision of information, or the production of identifiable documents embodying information, that the government may not withhold. Where documents include information which the government may withhold,[6] the court may permit the government, under the court's supervision, to excise such information. [Board Minutes, December 8-9, 1973, February 14, 1976.]

---

[1] The ACLU does not mean that all other forms of government concealment are proper. ACLU expresses no opinion on the legality of those activities which this statement would require to be disclosed. ACLU regards the issue of legality as a question separate from that of disclosure.

[2] The scope of the executive's obligation to make documents and information available to Congress, as distinct from the public at large, is the subject of a separate statement of policy. See section (e), below.

[3] The ACLU opposes the use of people in peacetime for the purpose of gathering foreign intelligence. See policy on Controlling the Intelligence Agencies.

[4] See also, ACLU policy on Governmental Surveillance.

[5] ACLU intends no implication that an injunction to protect properly withheld materials will ever be justified. The question of the appropriateness of criminal penalties for disclosure of properly withheld materials is a separate subject. In keeping with our long-standing policy against prior restraint, ACLU will continue to oppose any injunction to protect properly withheld materials.

[6] Such information may include information within the "advice privilege" (see below), or other information which an individual may have a right to insist be kept confidential on the ground that it is essentially personal. Whether the categories of privileged information established in the so-called Freedom of Information Act are too broad or too narrow are not considered in this statement, except, of course, for the category of information "specifically required by Executive order to be kept secret in the interest of the national defense or foreign policy." 5 U.S.C. § 552 (b)(1).

(See also policy on Government Defamation and Non-Disclosure, and on Controlling the Intelligence Agencies.)

***

(c) *Declassification*

The Union supports the establishment of an independent agency within the federal government to represent the public interest in the declassification of records hitherto kept secret and to work for increased disclosure. Such an agency should have authority to review and revise classification decisions made by the line agencies, which would, presumably, then exercise greater care and discrimination than is now the case. [Board Minutes, February 14, 1966.]

***

(d) *The "Pentagon Papers" Case*

One example of the Union's application of policy on access to government information is in its defense of publication by *The New York Times* of the so-called "Pentagon Papers," a study detailing the historical background of the political decisions from 1945-1968 which culminated in United States involvement in the Vietnam War.

Occurring in the midst of a national debate over the continuation of the war in Vietnam, the publication of the Defense Department's account of the process by which the United States became engaged militarily in Vietnam constituted a dissemination of information critically necessary for the proper functioning of a representative democracy. Indeed it is difficult to comprehend how a citizen can be expected to reach informed and rational decisions on the myriad issues raised by the war in Vietnam if he or she is denied access to the basic historical data relating to its origin.

It requires no great knowledge of either political science or constitutional law to recognize that information of the type which *The New York Times* published in this case constitutes the lifeblood of a functioning democracy. American courts have consistently emphasized that the free dissemination of information relevant to political questions of "public or general interest" is an indispensable pre-condition to effective representative democracy. [Board Minutes, June 18-19, 1977; ACLU amicus brief, *U.S.A. v. New York Times Company, et al.*; News Release, June 30, 1971.]

The abhorrence of prior restraint is firmly established in the law of the First Amendment. For reasons of overriding public importance, the Supreme Court has laid down the broad and immutable rule that government may not restrict free speech—particularly the dissemination of newspapers and periodicals—prior to publication. Nor can the ACLU condone government restraint which stops the presses to allow the courts to review what the newspapers want to publish (as occurred with *The New York Times'* publication of the "Pentagon Papers"). That would amount to a licensing system, which was precisely what the First Amendment was designed to avoid. [Board Minutes, June 18-19, 1977; ACLU amicus brief, *U.S.A. v. New York Times Company, et al.*; News Release, June 30, 1971.]

The ACLU believes that the disclosure of information which relates only to policies of previous administrations, which policies have been not only abandoned but expressly repudiated by the present government, cannot, as a matter of law, be prejudicial to the current and on-going security interests of this nation. [Board Minutes, June 18-19, 1977; ACLU amicus brief, *U.S.A. v. New York Times Company, et al.*; News Release, June 30, 1971.]

***

(e) Congress and the Advice Privilege (so-called executive privilege)

The right to know, in particular, the right of Congress to know, is fundamental. Congress, to perform its functions of enacting legislation and carrying on vigilant oversight of the administration of government, has the right to get information germane to a proper legislative inquiry.

The fact that the subject matter relates to foreign affairs or military affairs does not make it a subject of privilege.

No witness summoned by a congressional committee may refuse to appear on the ground that he or she intends to invoke the advice privilege as to all or some of the questions that may be asked.

The advice privilege may be claimed on behalf of a witness summoned by a congressional committee only at the direction of the President personally.

The advice privilege may be asserted only with respect to questions concerning recommendations, advice, and suggestions passed on for consideration in the formulation of governmental policy.

The advice privilege may not be asserted with respect to questions concerning what has been done, as distinct from what has been advised.

The advice privilege may not be asserted with respect to questions concerning facts acquired by the witness while acting in an official capacity.

The separation of "fact" from "advice," while sometimes difficult, is not impossible. Indeed, executive departments are often required by the courts to make this separation in order to comply with requests for documents under the Freedom of Information Act and other litigation. Without the separation, an advice privilege invites abuse.

Congress may require answers to questions about actions or advice by executive officials which it has probable cause to believe constitute criminal wrongdoing. In such situations, of course, individuals summoned before a congressional committee are entitled to exercise their constitutional rights, including, for example, the privilege against self-incrimination.[1]

The above guidelines apply to the assertion of the advice privilege to withhold documents[2] as well as personal testimony. Such documents may be withheld, pursuant to the privilege, only at the direction of the President

---

[1] The appearance of such witnesses before grand juries with respect to investigations of action or advice by executive officials which may constitute criminal wrongdoing raises separate questions not dealt with in this policy.

[2] "Documents" is intended to include any form of recorded information, such as tapes.

personally. The privilege extends not to entire documents, but only to those portions of documents which meet the criteria set out above to justify the advice privilege. [Board Minutes, December 8-9, 1973.]

***

(f) *Decision-making in Executive Session*

The ACLU believes that all meetings of any legislative or administrative body of the nation, state, city, or any subdivision thereof—including any board, commission, authority, council, agency, or committee, and also including sub-committees or subordinate groups of the above bodies—shall be open to the public. Meetings shall be defined as those gatherings of the body at which the official business of the body is or may be considered or transacted, including any informal or formal discussion, commitment, promise, consensus, decision or vote on any such business.

Each such body, where appropriate, shall have a regular schedule of meetings which shall be made public, and special meetings shall be held only upon reasonable notice to all members of such body and to the media. Minutes shall be taken of all open meetings, and the same shall be matters of public record. Minutes shall also be taken of all closed sessions and shall be available to any court reviewing the action of said body.

Closed sessions may be held (1) upon the majority vote of the body, conducted in public, following (2) a statement in general terms of the justification for such closed sessions, (3) to consider, but not otherwise to act, in the following instances only:

i. for the dismissal or disciplining of any non-elected public employee or licensed person, or investigation of charges against him or her, unless the person affected shall have requested an open meeting.

ii. for consideration of employment contracts, such as in collective bargaining;

iii. for discussion with legal counsel concerning matters which are or may be the subject of pending or imminent litigation in which the agency is or may be a party;

iv. where legitimately classified matters are under discussion (See section b of this policy);

v. in accordance with procedures comparable to those set forth in ACLU policy on Fair Legislative Procedures

Such closed sessions may not expand their discussions to include any other matter. [Board Minutes, December 7-8, 1974.]

***

Further Information (not policy)

The issue of prior restraint of the press was dealt with by the Supreme Court in the *Pentagon Papers* case. In *New York Times v. United States* (1971) the Court lifted the ban on publication because the government had failed to meet the heavy burden of justification necessary to defeat the strong presumption against the constitutional validity of any system of prior restraint. The seven concurring Justices each filed separate opinions, as did the three dissenters. Each separate opinion puts forward different grounds for the holding, and no one opinion represents the holding of the Court.

Under the Freedom of Information Act of 1966 and its 1975 amendments, records "specifically authorized under criteria established by an Executive order to be kept secret in the interest of national defense or foreign policy" and which are "in fact properly classified pursuant to such Executive order" can be withheld from the public. The Act gives to the courts the authority to examine anew the propriety of any such classified material, and requires the agency to show that the release of the information could be reasonably expected to cause damage to the national security.

The FOIA also permits federal agencies to withhold unclassified information concerning the following: matters concerning "internal personnel rules and practices" not affecting a member of the public; matters exempted from disclosure by statute; trade secrets and commercial or financial information given to an agency with the understanding that it shall be privileged or confidential; inter-agency or intra-agency communications revealing a person's opinions (but not facts); personnel and medical files and similar files whose disclosure would be a "clearly unwarranted invasion" of someone's privacy; reports prepared for or by an agency responsible for the regulation or supervision of financial institutions; and geological and geophysical data concerning wells.

Finally, the Act exempts from disclosure investigatory records compiled for law enforcement purposes whose release would meet one of the following conditions: 1) interfere with law enforcement, 2) deprive a person of a fair trial, 3) constitute an unwarranted invasion of personal privacy, 4) disclose the identity of a confidential source and, in criminal and lawful national security intelligence investigations, confidential information furnished only by such a source, 5) disclose investigative techniques, or 6) endanger the life or safety of law enforcement personnel.

Except for the above-mentioned exempted information, a federal agency must release to any member of the public who request it any documents from its records, subject to specified time limits and search fees. There are also special appeals procedures for dealing with agency refusals to release information.

The major Supreme Court decision affecting release of information to the public is *EPA v. Mink* (1973). The Court held that it could not review classification decisions because the FOIA specifically exempted classified materials. However, as noted above, the 1975 amendment to the FOIA now permits courts to determine whether information is "properly classified."

In a series of cases the Supreme Court has considered a number of the specific exemptions to the FOIA.

In *Renegotiation Board v. Bannercraft Clothing Co., Inc.* (1974), the Court held that 1) the Renegotiation Board is not exempt from FOIA because it is an agency within the meaning of the Act; 2) in a renegotiation case the contractor is required to pursue its administrative remedy and may not, if it fails to do so, attain its ends through the judicial process. In *Renegotiation Board v. Grumman Aircraft* (1975), the Court held that the reports of the Regional Board of Renegotiation and a division of the Renegotiation Board (consisting of 3-5 members), which were submitted to the "full" Renegotiation Board for a final decision on whether excess profits had been realized, were not final decisions and therefore fall within Exemption 5 to FOIA (exempting interagency or intra-agency memorandums which would not be available by law to a party other than an agency in litigation with the agency).

In *National Labor Relations Board v. Sears Roebuck and Co..* (1975), the Court held that the "Advice and Appeals Memoranda" that explain decisions by the N.L.R.B. General Counsel not to file a complaint are final opinions within the FOIA and thereby are not within the scope of the attorney work product exemption to the FOIA (Exemption 5).

In *Administrator, Federal Aviation Administration v. Robertson* (1975), the Court held that reports of the Federal Aviation Administration consisting of the Agency's analysis of the operation and maintenance performance of commercial airlines are exempt from public disclosure under Exemption 3 of the FOIA (specifically exempted from disclosure by statute) because Congress did not intend in the FOIA to repeal all prior specific exemptions. Hence Section 1104 of the Federal Aviation Act of 1958, providing for withholding of the reports in this case, justified nondisclosure.

In *Department of the Air Force v. Rose* (1976), the Court considered whether case summaries of honor and ethics hearings were exempt from disclosure under the FOIA. The Court held that the exemption for internal personnel rules and practices of an agency did not apply because Congress intended this exemption to draw a line between trivial matters and substantial matters in which the public might have a leigitimate interest. The substantive role of the Air Force and its academy and the case summaries was held to be such a substantial matter. The Court further held that Exemption 6 to the FOIA-personnel, medical and similar files, was designed to prevent against unwarranted invasions of personal privacy as distinguished from a blanket exemption for such files: the editing of documents to prevent such intrusions can serve this purpose and thus the materials are not exempt in toto.

In *United States v. Nixon* (1974), the Court considered former President Nixon's assertion of an unqualified Presidential privilege of immunity from judicial process in the context of a subpoena for certain tapes and documents issued in a criminal proceeding. The Court held that the President's generalized assertion of a privilege must yield to the specific need for evidence in a pending criminal trial and the demands of due process, at least absent a claim of need to protect military or diplomatic secrets.

Census Questions

The inclusion in the decennial census of questions pertaining to race and ethnicity raises problems for civil libertarians. A difficult conflict exists between the right of privacy and the government's need for information on which to base legislation and programs to support and implement other fundamental rights, such as freedom from discrimination. At the time of the 1970 decennial census, the ACLU, believing that data about race and ethnic groupings in the U.S. population have a clear social utility, supported the policy of the Bureau of the Census to include questions on race and ethnicity. However, we urged that answers to questions on race and ethnicity be voluntary, because of 1) the existence of real and justifiable fears by persons asked to designate their racial or ethnic origins, and 2) the loose and unscientific concepts of race and ethnic origins used at that time by the Bureau. We also urged that, in order to protect the "equally compelling" right of privacy, the Bureau continue its "excellent" past record of protecting the confidentiality of individual responses.

In the years since the last census, we have become increasingly sensitive to the right of privacy. In particular, we oppose the arrangement which presently exists between the Census Bureau and the National Archives. Under the arrangement, 72 years after the census, when it is presumed that the privacy interests of the individuals counted are no longer compelling, the Archives discloses records, including personal identifying information, to anyone who presents him/herself as a researcher or historian. Thus, the 1910 census records are due to be made available in 1982.

The ACLU opposes disclosure of identifiable census records by the National Archives or by others. The ACLU believes such disclosure violates the agreement of confidentiality made when the census count is taken. This position is prompted by the Archives/Census Bureau arrangement and the increasing technological potential for invasion of privacy. While we believe that government ought to make every reasonable effort to obtain information which serves the "clear social utility" set forth above, all answers to census questions should be made on a voluntary basis, except that:

1) ACLU does not object to the Census Bureau requirement that names and addresses be given on a compulsory basis because, were only voluntary answers permitted, serious statistical inaccuracies could occur. Indeed, information concerning name and address is all that is needed to serve the purpose of the Census as described in the Constitution, that of determining proportionate Congressional representation.

2) The government may collect information pertaining to race and ethnicity or any other matter only where it is assembled in a manner which protects the privacy of individuals by separating the racial or ethnic information from personal identifying information such as name and address. [Board Minutes, September 24-25, 1977.]

Finally, the ACLU opposes the inclusion of any question relating to religious affiliation or belief, whether on a compulsory or voluntary basis, in the decennial census or interdecennial sample survey, or in any comprehensive survey conducted by the government. This is because the First Amendment, which prohibits a governmental establishment of religion and guarantees the free exercise of religion, prevents the government from putting to any use the information on religion that it might collect. Even the expression of government interest in the religious activities of the population is an intrusion into the province of religious privacy. [Board Minutes, December 2-3, 1967.]

***

Further Information (not policy)

In *United States v. Steele* (1972), the United States Court of Appeals for the Ninth Circuit reversed the conviction of a member of a census resistance movement who was convicted under a statute governing refusal or neglect to answer questions on a census form. There was a showing that at least six other persons violated the statute, but were not prosecuted and that background reports were compiled only on persons who publicly attacked the census. The government offered no justification other than prosecutorial discretion. The court found purposeful discrimination in the enforcement of the statute.

Policy #9

Copyrights

The question of the right of government employees to copyright published materials developed during the course of their employment raises a possible civil liberties issue if, as has been suggested, the copyright is in some circumstances meant to serve as a deliberate and calculated device to restrict the dissemination of information.

Actual government publications normally should not be subject to copyright. If any exceptions are allowed, they must be carefully circumscribed to permit the widest possible distribution of information by the government.

However, the copyright law should not be interpreted to curtail the right of government employees to write, on their own time and for their own profit, about their official work. [Board Minutes, June 18-19, 1977.]

Policy #13

Government Pressures on Newspapers

(a) The First Amendment, by which diversity of opinion is protected, constitutes no bar to investigation of economic concentration in the newspaper field under the anti-trust acts. The ACLU is opposed, however, to investigation political and social opinions. [Board Minutes, December 17, 1962, January 21, 1963.]

***

(b) A law prohibiting all electioneering on election day, including such forms of expression as newspaper editorials, is too sweeping in its incursions of the freedoms of speech and of the press to be justified by its stated purposes of preventing the disruption of honest elections. Such a law errs both in defining too vaguely the evil to be combatted and in prescribing a remedy which violates constitutionally guaranteed freedoms without any showing of a "clear and present danger" that the exercise of these freedoms will bring about a specific evil result. [Board Minutes, June 18-19, 1977.]

***

Further Information (not policy)

In *Mills v. Alabama* (1966),the Supreme Court struck down a criminal statute which prohibited the solicitation of votes on election day. Such a statute was held to abridge the guarantee of a free press by inhibiting free discussion of political and government affairs.

Policy #35

Congressional Expression

(a) The Union opposes any constitutional amendment nullifying the principle of congressional immunity and thus restricting full freedom of debate in Congress. It also opposes any legislation making the government itself liable for damages sustained by any person as a result of a libel or slander made by a member of Congress under his or her personal immunity. Defamatory statements made in Congress may be deplorable, but they are a necessary hazard of democracy if congressional debate is to remain truly unrestricted.

However, the Union recognizes the need for congressional responsibility and suggests that this be achieved by voluntary measures of congressional self-discipline. Such measures should include the provision of a forum in which an accused person may rebut the charges, a method by which a person slandered may enter a reply in the *Congressional Record*, and the spontaneous denunciation of defamatory tactics by other members of Congress at the time such incidents occur. [Board Minutes, March 5, 1951; News Release, July 31, 1951.]

***

(b) Because of its long devotion to and deep concern for freedom of expression, the ACLU is unalterably opposed to the practice of filibustering. The purpose of free speech, particularly speech expressing a minority view, is to help in the formation of a wise decision by the majority. A filibuster constitutes nothing less than the frustration of that majority will by a minority. [Board Minutes, September 24-25, 1977.]

Debate on any bill is necessary to clarify its meaning and content, so that when the time comes to vote on the measure, both legislators and citizens will be better informed about the scope, content, and probable effects of the proposed legislation. But after the bill has been thoroughly explained and commented on, further consideration passes the point of debate and becomes a filibuster, no longer serving to elucidate the issues but designed only to prevent the legislative body from voting. It is no longer an exercise in freedom of speech but simply an open effort to thwart legislative decision-making. In such circumstances the Union urges that closure be invoked. [Board Minutes, September 24-25, 1977.]

***

(c) A duly elected member of a legislative body cannot be denied his or her seat because of expressions of disagreement with United States laws or policies. Such denial infringes the member's freedom of expression and subjects the individual in effect to trial by the legislature without the constitutionally guaranteed protection of trial by jury. Moreover, the voter is unconstitutionally deprived of the right to vote by the ouster of his or her elected representative. [Board Minutes, September 24-25, 1977.]

***

Further Information (not policy)

In *Gravel v. United States* (1972), the Supreme Court permitted a grand jury investigating the release of the classified "Pentagon Papers" to question an aide of a senator who had placed the unabridged text of the study in the *Congressional Record* and who arranged for private publication. The majority distinguished between acts that are "legislative" in nature and therefore entitled to protection, and those "non-legislative" acts not entitled to constitutional immunity. The Constitution's free speech and debate clause's grant of legislative immunity was held to apply to activities that are "an integral part of the deliberative and communicative processes by which members participate in committee and House proceedings with respect to the consideration and passage or rejection of proposed legislation or other matters which the Constitution places within the jurisdiction of either House." The Court concluded that neither the private republication of the papers nor their acquisition by Senator Gravel's aide met this test, but the act of inserting the papers into the *Congressional Record* was held to be constitutionally protected. The Court found no constitutional or other privilege protecting a legislator or his aide from being forced to disclose sources of information before a grand jury investigation, if that information might prove relevant to uncovering crimes by third parties and "as long as no legislative act is implicated by the questions."

In *Powell v. McCormack* (1969), the Supreme Court held that the House of Representatives was without power to exclude from its membership any person who was duly elected by his constituents and who met the constitutional age, citizenship and residency requirements, and found the case a justiciable one rather than one involving a non-justiciable political question. The Court held that while the speech and debate clause's grant of legislative immunity precluded Representative Adam Clayton Powell from suing House Speaker McCormack for illegally voting to exclude him from office, the congressional doorkeeper and paymaster could be prevented from executing the House's illegal order.

In *Eastland v. United States Serviceman's Fund* (1975), members and the chief counsel of a congressional subcommittee were held to be immune from a suit to enjoin enforcement of a subpoena issued by the subcommittee which was alleged to infringe upon First Amendment rights. The *Eastland* test appears to be that when the actions directed by Congress or its subcommittees are "essential to legislating," their validity cannot be examined by the judiciary.

In *McClellan v. McSurely*, a Federal District Court ruled that Senate subcommittee investigators, who, without court approval, examined and received photocopies of personal property seized in violation of the Fourth Amendment were not immune under the speech and debate clause's grant of legislative immunity from suit for damages. Nor was the senator for whom they were working. On appeal, the United States Court of Appeals for the District of Columbia Circuit affirmed by an equally divided court. In October 1977, the United States Supreme Court granted certiorari to consider the issues.

Policy #37

Financial Disclosure Requirements of Government Officials
A conflict exists between the need for public information about government operations and protection of the individual government employee's[1] right of privacy and freedom of association. Both are civil liberties interests.

A balancing of these conflicting interests requires that disclosure requirements 1) apply only to employees working in positions that closely affect the public welfare, whose functions involve a substantial possibility of a conflict or other impropriety, and to candidates for such positions, and 2) require the disclosure only of such financial or other information as is reasonably necessary for the public discovery of such a conflict or impropriety or appearance of such a conflict or impropriety.

The ACLU opposes broad, general disclosure requirements, but does not oppose requirements that relate to particular jobs and that require particular information. A decision on when the ACLU will support or oppose such requirements must be made in the individual case on the basis of the guidelines presented above. [Board Minutes, October 2-3, 1976.]

[1] The term "government employee" includes all employees of every state, local, or federal government, whether elected, appointed or otherwise.

Assembly and Public Protest

Policy #39

Civil Disobedience, Picketing, and Demonstrations

(a) In the past few years particularly, the ACLU has been confronted by situations in which individuals have violated laws of the United States or of its states or municipalities and have requested ACLU defense in connection with the violation. These cases have presented the ACLU with a complex and troublesome issue. In many cases those who have violated such laws have done so primarily because they wished by their disobedience to express their views on some aspect of public life. Some have labeled their behavior "civil disobedience."

Many different types of acts have been called "civil disobedience," and we should therefore make clear our definition of the term. Generally speaking, civil disobedience is the willful, nonviolent and public violation of valid laws because the violator deems them to be unjust or because their violation will focus public attention on other injustices in society to which such laws may or may not be related. Some people include as a form of civil disobedience the violation of federal or state laws or municipal ordinances which themselves violate the United States Constitution. The ACLU has defended individuals who disobey state and local laws and ordinances that perpetuate segregation in public schools or public transportation because this is an appropriate and traditional method of challenging such legislation. The ACLU will continue to defend individuals who violate laws which, either in themselves or as applied in the circumstances, the ACLU believes to be unconstitutional or to interfere with the exercise of constitutional right, whether or not the courts have previously ruled otherwise, or whether or not such violations are called civil disobedience. The considerations which move people to challenge the constitutionality of legislation by violating such laws are different from the impetus to protest "unjust" but clearly valid laws by disobeying them.

Civil disobedience does not occur when people surreptitiously violate laws, as by exceeding speed limits. In these cases, there is no attempt to bring to the public's attention the "injustice" of a valid law. Again, civil disobedience is not involved when one inadvertently violates a law, like forgetting to include savings account interest in one's tax return. The public protest element is missing in such instances, too. Open rebellion or riots, like those which occurred in Watts, California and have occurred in a number of American cities recently, are not examples of civil disobedience since they involve violence and are not peaceful attempts to focus attention on injustice by persuading the public to change unjust laws.

We believe there are two broad categories to which the term "civil disobedience" is properly applied. The first involves the deliberate violation of a law because the individual believes the law itself is unjust even though it is constitutional. The second category of civil disobedience arises when an individual violates a valid law with which the person has no quarrel but does so to protest or call attention to some other evil which may or may not be related to the law which is being violated.

Many of the people who have been involved in either type of civil disobedience have willingly submitted to arrest, prosecution, and imprisonment because they believe the theory of civil disobedience requires their acceptance of the consequences of their illegal conduct as proof of their respect for society as a whole and for its laws in general. This was the view of Dr. Martin Luther King. In these cases, the ACLU has little, if any, role to play. Our concern arises when those who violate valid laws seek our assistance in order to avoid the law's consequences on the grounds that they acted out of conscience or deeply felt convictions and should avoid punishment because of their motivation.

In both types of civil disobedience, many of those who have violated laws have acted out of the highest principle, often out of asserted compliance with obligations of conscience and to accomplish a purpose with which decent people may agree—to end discrimination, to clean up the slums, to protest against wars. Nevertheless, the ACLU believes that no civil liberties issue is presented if the violators are arrested, prosecuted, and punished, bearing in mind that due process must be afforded in the arrest and prosecution and that equal protection of the laws must be accorded with respect to the bail set or punishment meted out. Specifically, the right to counsel must be provided, the trial held in an atmosphere that is not prejudicial to the rights of the accused, and the sentence imposed not more severe than would be imposed on another person who violated the same law. We have been concerned that more severe sentences have been imposed on persons who have openly violated laws they deemed unjust than those imposed on others who commit violations of the same laws for anti-social reasons. Indeed, the fact that peaceful, nonviolent behavior was involved in the violation of a law should be taken into account by the court in considering the sentence to be imposed, even though such factors are not relevant to the question of guilt or innocence with respect to the offense involved. Furthermore, we will continue to oppose the improper application or over-energetic enforcement of disorderly conduct, trespass, and similar ordinances where the right of protest is involved and where the inconvenience is minor. The right to free speech and to hold peaceful meetings and demonstrations will continue to be defended by the ACLU.

However, the ACLU believes that freedom to say what one believes, not do what one wishes, is what is protected by the First Amendment. High motivation and deep-felt conscience may be, and often are, the moving force of those who practice civil disobedience. But this does not mean that those who disobey laws for baser principles or less altruistic motives should be convicted while those who deliberately disobey laws for better-motivated reasons should be acquitted.

To make this type of distinction would be to change a nation governed by law to one governed by motivation alone. Indeed, conscience can lead people to good or evil—assuming society is able to distinguish between conscience and baser motivations.

It is not the ACLU's function to decide whether history will determine that an individual who disobeyed a specific valid law at a particular time helped or hurt humanity. Nor need we judge whether those who practice civil disobedience, and willingly accept punishment therefor, are more responsible and consistently devoted to their principles than those who, having violated valid laws, seek ACLU assistance to avoid the consequences of their violation. Nor is it our province to raise the question of whether civil disobedience is the only or the best or wisest method of persuading the public that a particular law is unjust.

For us, the single question is whether the act involved is the violation of a valid law or one we believe is invalid. In the latter case, we will defend the violation of law; otherwise we will not.

It should be understood that nothing in this statement is intended to change the ACLU practice on moral grounds, on appropriate occasions, of urging authorities to extend leniency in sentencing or imposing disciplinary measures, or in seeking pardons or amnesty. Where there is no ground for legal defense on the merits, considerations of mercy, compassion or justice should often be extended even to those who have acted illegally either because of religious or ethical convictions or to dramatize what they believe to be serious social evils. Such a policy would not ordinarily cover acts of violence or coercion nor serious denial of the rights or liberties of others. [Board Minutes, October 5-6, 1968.]

***

(b) Picketing is an expression of the rights of free speech and assembly protected by the First Amendment. The ACLU supports the right to picket in any circumstances, by any method, in any numbers, with the limitations only that picketing shall not be accompanied by fraudulent or libelous signs, violence by those demonstrating, or obstruction of streets and highways or of the place being picketed. Neither the merits of the controversy nor the wisdom of picketing in any particular case affects in any way the constitutional right to picket. [Board Minutes, February 14, 1938; News Release, January 21, 1946.] POLICY UNDER REVIEW.

Orderly, non-violent protests such as "sit-ins" are not a trespass on private property but rather an exercise of the constitutional right to express opinion. [Board Minutes, February 28, 1960, March 28, 1960; News Release, April 14, 1960.]

POLICY UNDER REVIEW.

Picketing of the White House may not be excluded from the protection of the First Amendment, since such activity can have no direct intimidatory effect on the judicial process. [Board Minutes, September 24-25, 1977.]

(See also policy on Picketing in section on Labor-Business, on Private

Pressure Groups for a discussion of primary and secondary boycotts in non-labor issues, and on Attempts To Influence Courts.)

***

(c) The right of assembly may be regulated only to protect the public's substantive rights, not merely to avoid inconvenience. A permit may be required for the holding of parades and public meetings, and meetings and demonstrations may be regulated, for example, to prevent undue restriction of normal traffic or to limit use of facilities to one group at a time. But this power may not be used, through *ex parte* injunctions or any other means, to "protect" the public from exposure to what some members of the public, or some officials, do not want said.

It is the duty of the government not only to refrain from interference with peaceful assemblies but also to restrain those citizens who would themselves suppress such demonstrations. This task is particularly incumbent upon governors, mayors, and police officials. The courts have plainly declared that important constitutional rights such as free speech and assembly and equal protection of the laws cannot be curtailed because of mere *apprehension* that the exercise of these rights will result in riotous disturbances by lawless opponents. It is up to the police to prevent hostile threats against peaceful demonstrators and to arrest those seeking to break up an assembly. [Board Minutes, September 24-25, 1977.]

(See also policy on College Students' Civil Liberties for discussion of campus demonstrations.)

***

Further Information (not policy)

The Supreme Court has made rulings in a number of cases affecting demonstrations and picketing. In *Shuttlesworth v. City of Birmingham, Alabama* (1969) the Court reiterated its hostility to permit systems which fail to articulate with precision the basis on which a permit is to be granted or withheld. In effect, the Court noted, a vague and standardless permit system vests a petty local official with unrestrained discretion to censor public expression. *Gregory et al. v. City of Chicago* (1969) reversed a decision of the Illinois Supreme Court sustaining the conviction of demonstrators picketing in front of Mayor Daley's home for the desegregation of Chicago schools. The Supreme Court held that the demonstrators had been convicted for holding the demonstration and that the peaceful and orderly march fell within the sphere of conduct protected by the First Amendment.

In *Coates v. City of Cincinnati* (1971) the Court held that an ordinance making it an offense for "three or more persons to assemble on any of the sidewalks and there conduct themselves in a manner annoying to persons passing by" violates the constitutional right of free assembly and association. Mere public intolerance or animosity cannot be the basis for abridgement of these constitutional freedoms. *Cohen v. California* (1971) extended the scope of constitutional protection to vulgar and profane language. Although the Court has held that the states are free to ban the use of so-called "fighting words," the four-letter word displayed by Cohen in relation to the draft was clearly not, in this instance, "directed to the person of the hearer."

Police Dept. of Chicago v. Mosley (1972) avoided the issue of whether a sidewalk abutting a public school could be placed off-limits to a solitary picket causing no disturbance by ruling that, because labor picketing would be permitted on the site, Chicago was in violation of the equal principle and its statute was facially unconstitutional.

In *Jeannette Rankin Brigade v. Chief of Capitol Police* (1972) the Court affirmed a ruling of a three-judge court that governmental interest in maintenance of a "park-like setting" on capitol grounds was not sufficient to sustain a statute prohibiting parades or assemblages on the capitol grounds. *Papachristou v. City of Jacksonville, Florida* (1972) held that various vagrancy provisions were too vague and indefinite to serve as the basis for prohibiting certain forms of assembly, and gave undue discretion to law enforcement officers.

Policy #41

Sound Truck, Solicitation and Literature Regulation

(a) The right of free speech implies another right—the right of the individual to choose to listen or not to listen. But there will be occasions on which these two rights come into direct conflict and some accommodation must be found. Such a problem is raised by the operation of sound trucks in the public streets. The Union believes that sound trucks may be regulated as to the time, place, and volume of their operation, but they may not be altogether banned or subject to unreasonable restrictions. [Board Minutes, January 23, 1950.]

(See also policy on Transit Radio.]
***

(b) Although public solicitation of money may be subject to reasonable regulation, to ban it altogether is a violation of civil liberties because solicitation is so often an essential feature of political agitation and a method of transmission of ideas as important as speech itself. [Board Minutes, April 3, 1950.]
***

(c) No license should be necessary for the free distribution or even the sale of literature, commercial or non-commercial, in public places or by house-to-house distribution. Printed matter is always protected by the constitutional guarantee of freedom of the press that sets it apart from the sale of ordinary goods. If the distribution of material expressing opinion can be restricted by license requirements merely because it is sold, then many organizations which cannot afford to distribute free literature will be seriously hampered. [Board Minutes, August 24, 1941; Weekly Bulletin, September 8, 1941.]

Equally improper is the effort to prevent house-to-house distribution of literature by means of anti-litter ordinances. [Board Minutes, September 24-25, 1977.]

POLICY UNDER REVIEW, along with other policies pertaining to the "captive audience" problem.

***

Further Information (not policy)

Cohen v. California (1971) concerned the conviction of a young man pursuant to a statute which prohibited disturbing the peace or quiet of any neighborhood or person by offensive conduct. The Supreme Court upheld the free speech right of the individual over the privacy right of the "captives." The "conduct" in question was the wearing of a jacket with the words, "Fuck the Draft," printed on it. The Court said: "Much has been made of the claim that Cohen's distasteful mode or expression was thrust upon unwilling or unsuspecting viewers, and that the State might therefore legitimately act as it did in order to protect the sensitive from otherwise unavoidable exposure to appellant's crude form of protest . . . While this Court has recognized that government may properly act in many situations to prohibit intrusion into the privacy of the home . . . we have at the same time consistently stressed that we are often 'captives' outside the sanctuary of the home and subject to objectional speech . . . The ability of government, consonant with the Constitution, to shut off discourse solely to protect others from hearing it is, in other words, dependent upon a showing that substantial privacy interests are being invaded in an essentially intolerable manner."

In *Lehman v. City of Shaker Heights* (1974) the Supreme Court held that a city could prohibit all political advertisements from placards on transit trains. The Court emphasized the commercial aspect of the transit venture, asserting that the city would jeopardize the chance of getting revenue from long-term contracts with advertisers if political advertisement were displayed on the cars.

Erznoznik v. City of Jacksonville (1975) concerned a challenge to the validity of a Jacksonville, Fla. ordinance that prohibited showing films containing nudity by a drive-in movie theater when its screen is visible from a public street or place. The statute was not claimed to be within the permissible restraints on obscenity. In its decision the Court said: "A state or municipality may protect individual privacy by enacting reasonable time, place, and manner regulations applicable to all speech irrespective of content. . . . But when the government acting as a censor, undertakes selectively to shield the public from some kinds of speech on the grounds that they are more offensive than others, the First Amendment strictly limits its power . . . Such selective restrictions have been upheld only when the speaker intrudes on the privacy of the home or the degree of captivity makes it impractical for the unwilling viewer or auditor to avoid exposure."

The Ultra-Right

(a) In those communities where members of the police force are also members of the John Birch Society, the ACLU reaffirms its position that mere membership in any organization is not sufficient grounds for disqualification from public employment. The judgment of people on the basis of their individual ability and competence, not on their political beliefs and associations, is a cardinal civil liberties principle which supports the First Amendment guarantee of freedom of expression. The right to associate for lawful purposes is a constitutionally protected right, and no public servant should be barred from exercising it.

Certainly public authorities should have discretion to inquire into the suitability of any member of the police force at any time, especially when they receive any information which they think may reflect on the member's capability to perform police duties. Such information might include personal activity as a member of the John Birch Society which is shown to have interfered with the impartial conduct we expect law enforcement officers to demonstrate in the exercise of their authority. But the guiding standard for such inquiry should be personal activity, not mere membership. [Board Minutes, December 21, 1964.]

***

(b) Because the Union opposes any governmental interference with the private associations and beliefs—however extreme, distorted, or obnoxious—of any citizen, it opposes government investigation of the John Birch Society, the Ku Klux Klan, the American Nazi Party, or any other extremist groups. Such governmental investigations are unwise not only because they thrust a governmental body into the delicate area of First Amendment freedoms, but also because they tend to create a public climate of fear and intimidation in which free speech and association of all kinds are inhibited. Recognizing that such groups are frequently guilty of assaulting the First Amendment freedoms of others, the Union nevertheless believes that the only proper way to fight such assaults is for persons of opposing views to refute their attacks by counter speech in the public arena.

Although the democratic standards in which the ACLU believes and for which it fights run directly counter to the philosophy of the Klan and other ultra-right groups, the vitality of the democratic institutions the ACLU defends lies in their equal application to all.

The government may not investigate the philosophy of any group, but it may investigate and prosecute any acts of physical harassment or violence by ultra-right groups which violate criminal laws. The Department of Justice has the authority to enforce these laws. Any investigation of the Department's enforcement action would be the responsibility of the House Judiciary Committee. [Board Minutes, September 24-25, 1977.]

(See also part c, below, for discussion of the Union's own strategy in combatting the activities of ultra-right groups.)

***

(c) In dealing with the problem of extremist organizations the Union is confronted with the difficult dilemma of having to defend the civil liberties of groups whose activities do fundamental injury to civil liberties. These guidelines should be followed:

1) The right of all groups to express their opinions must be defended regardless of the point of view they express.

2) The ACLU does not comment on any part of the content of the ultra-right groups' programs which does not directly concern civil liberties, whether it be repeal of the income tax, the social security program, or removal of the United Nations from New York City.

3) However, when an ultra-right group espouses positions adversely affecting civil liberties—for example, efforts to remove a teacher because of the teacher's "liberal" views, or attacks on librarians for refusing to take "Communist" books off library shelves—the Union should vigorously present its position, while defending the group's right to speak. (See also policy on Pressure Group Attacks on Schools and Libraries.) The Union should also emphasize the point that the loose accusations of these groups can create an atmosphere of caution in which dissident views will not be expressed. [Board Minutes, September 24-25, 1977.]

Policy #51

ACLU and Intra-Labor Conflicts

The ACLU will participate in cases of intra-labor union conflict where it is found that the procedure used in disciplining an individual member has not met the minimum standards of due process. Cases of this kind would not go to the merits of the dispute but only to the form of the procedure itself. The ACLU could act on several levels, from negotiation with the offending union to, as a last resort, a suit on behalf of the injured party.

Where the charges against an individual are claimed to be merely a subterfuge to penalize a member or members for activity which is entirely legitimate but which is noxious to the union leadership, the ACLU is in a more difficult position, since the charges may be technically tenable, the evidence ample, and the procedure scrupulous. If the charges are a screen to rid the union of dissidents, the ACLU will act. This is a violation of civil liberties.

Cases involving substantive policy issues within trade unions—such as measures by the union leadership to discipline union members for activity which it believes inimical to the union—will be treated just like any other substantive issue which comes before the ACLU for resolution.

In those cases where the law vests the Secretary of Labor with authority to act in cases of alleged wrongdoings by labor unions, the ACLU will call this to the attention of the victim, and, in appropriate cases, urge the Secretary of Labor to act. [Board Minutes, September 24-25, 1977.]

POLICY UNDER REVIEW, along with other labor policies.

Policy #52

Union and Corporation Political Activity

(a) The ACLU supports the prohibition of contributions to election campaigns by business corporations and associations and by labor unions from union treasury funds. [Board Minutes, February 9-10, 1974.]

***

(b) Expenditures by labor unions and corporations for other political purposes, including the expression of views on and support of legislative and social issues, are a proper exercise of the rights of free expression protected by the First Amendment. There should be no absolute prohibition against such expression, but reasonable limitations may properly be set by statute as to the total amount expended. This is particularly necessary to prevent evasion of the law by multiplying what is essentially a single source. [Board Minutes, May 28, 1962, February 9-10, 1974.] (See also, policy on Contributions and Expenditures for Election Campaigns.)

***

(c) Requiring individual workers who have chosen not to be members of a union to support financially the political activities of the union is a violation of the individual's political freedom.

Requiring individual workers to contribute financially through labor unions to political candidates' campaigns to which they do not wish to contribute is a violation of the individual's political freedom. This applies both to members and to those who have chosen not to be members. Union funds should be allocated or assessed for political campaigns only in ways that provide reasonable opportunities for workers to certify that they object to such expenditures and not to contribute to them. [Board Minutes, February 17-18, 1973.] (See also policy on Closed Shop, Union Shop, and Right to Work Laws.)

***

(d) The First Amendment is not violated by the refusal of the Internal Revenue Service to recognize a tax deduction claim for money spent by business corporations for political activities whose purpose is the preservation of a vital business interest. [Board Minutes, September 11, 1961.]

***

(e) The ACLU recognizes the union member's responsibility to avoid actions directly detrimental to the union, but upholds the right generally to take part in public debate—and the public's right to hear such comment. A union may not justifiably expel a member for openly expressing political opinions at variance with those of the union leadership. Where the relationship between advocacy of an idea and the union's well-being is itself highly debatable, disciplinary proceedings should be closely limited, lest they silence the member's expression of views within the range of fair discussion. The burden of establishing the gravity of the offense should rest on the union. [Board Minutes, September 24-25, 1977.]

Policy #57

Academic Freedom in the New Colleges

(a) Responsible governance of a college or university today must embrace real support for such essential principles of academic freedom as tenure, substantive and procedural due process, and freedom of expression and association. Because the ideals of scholarship can be pursued effectively only in an atmosphere of intellectual freedom, the ACLU suggests that accrediting associations emphasize these minimal academic freedom standards as criteria for granting, continuing, or discontinuing accreditation in institutions of higher learning. [Board Minutes, December 13, 1966.]

***

(b) The newly established college faces particularly heavy responsibilities and problems in its efforts to win accreditation, recognition, support, and independence from unwarranted pressures, and to create a climate favorable to freedom for teaching, for research, and for learning. In addition to standards of academic freedom and due process for teachers set forth above in parts a, b, c and d of the policy on Teachers' Freedom and Responsibility and Due Process in Higher Education (and for students, as described in policy on College Students' Civil Liberties), special attention must be given to the following:

1) Is there significant participation of faculty in major policy decisions on curriculum and personnel, including appointment, promotion, and dismissal?

2) May faculty tenure be attained after a limited period of probation?

3) Are there specific regulations governing non-reappointment and resignation? [Minutes of Academic Freedom Committee, January 12, 1965; Statement on the New College, October 1965.]

Teachers' Rights in Primary and Secondary Education

(a) In general, the rights of teachers in secondary schools are the same as the rights of teachers in colleges and universities (see policy on Teachers' Freedom and Responsibility and Due Process in Higher Education). Of particular relevance to teachers in secondary schools are the following principles:

The professional staff, by virtue of its training and experience, has the right and responsibility to establish the curriculum, subject to the approval of boards of education and state departments of education. Within the individual classroom, the teacher should be given reasonable scope in the implementation of the designated objectives, content, and methods of the curriculum, and in the choice of supplementary material other than textbooks. When a controversial issue is studied, conflicting points of view should be explored. The teacher has the right to identify and express his or her own point of view in the classroom as long as it is indicated clearly that it is the teacher's own. Where parents, as individuals, or parent or other community groups raise the question of suitability of any material, out of concern for maturity level, morality, patriotism, literary merit, etc., the decision as to its acceptability should be vested in a representative professional committee. (See policy on Selection of School and Library Materials and Pressure Group Attacks.)

At faculty conferences and meetings teachers have the right to express opinions on school policies and conditions, to make declarations, and to vote on issues without fear of reprisals. Teachers have the right to meet privately without the presence of administrative staff, and to disseminate their views either as individuals or groups. They may join unions and may exercise the right to strike. (See policy on Government Employment.)

A teacher should be free to conduct himself or herself outside the academic setting as he or she sees fit, unless it can be shown that the behavior is affecting professional performance in a demonstrably deleterious manner. [Board Minutes, May 9, 1968; *Academic Freedom in the Secondary Schools*, 1968.]

(See also policy on Loyalty Oaths.)

***

(b) The ACLU affirms support for the principle of tenure for teachers in elementary and secondary schools.

The ACLU affirms its support for equal protection, due process and academic freedom principles embodied in the concept of tenure and urges application of these principles for all tenured and non-tenured primary and secondary teachers. [Board Minutes, April 8-9, 1972.]

POLICY UNDER REVIEW.

***

Further Information (not policy)

In the landmark case of *Keyishian v. Board of Regents* (1967), the Supreme Court struck down the Feinberg Law, a New York statute which required teachers to sign loyalty oaths as a prerequisite of employment and which disqualified all members of the Communist Party from academic employment. The statute was held to be unconstitutionally overbroad and vague, resulting in the "chilling of the exercise of vital First Amendment rights." The Court emphasized that public employment, including academic employment, may not be conditioned upon the surrender of constitutional rights and found that the statute "[swept] overbroadly into association which cannot be proscribed."

In *Pickering v. Board of Education* (1968), a teacher challenged his dismissal for writing a letter to a newspaper attacking the school board's handling of financial matters. The Supreme Court majority concluded that absent proof of "false statements knowingly or reckless made by him," a teacher's exercise of his First Amendment right to contribute to public debate may not constitute a basis for dismissal from public employment.

In the *Roth* and *Sinderman* cases in 1972 the Supreme Court held that tenured teachers had a right to a due process hearing before dismissal. Probationary contractual teachers had no general right to a hearing challenging a decision not to renew their contract. But all teachers, tenured and non-tenured, had the right to due process if the decision to dismiss or not to renew was based upon exercise of constitutional rights or would result in unconstitutional discrimination. In effect, the non-tenured teacher had first to demonstrate that the adverse decision did infringe constitutional rights before a hearing was required.

In February 1977, the Supreme Court vacated and remanded a U.S. Court of Appeals for the Sixth Circuit decision reinstating and awarding back pay to an untenured high school teacher because the school board's decision to fire him was found to be based in "substantial part" on the teacher's communication with a local radio station about the school's dress code. In *Mount Healthy School District v. Doyle* (1977), the Supreme Court, while agreeing that the teacher's claims were not defeated because he was untenured, and that the communication was protected conduct under the First and Fourteenth Amendments, held that the district court should have examined whether, by a preponderance of the evidence, the Board would have reached its decision not to renew the contract absent the protected conduct.

Policy #60

Release of Information about Students

(a) The essential safeguard of academic freedom is mutual trust and the realization by both student and teacher that their freedoms are reciprocal. Any abrogation of or restriction on the academic freedom of the one, will inevitably, adversely affect the other. Because the student-teacher relationship is a privileged one, the student does not expect that the view he or she expresses, either orally or in writing, and either in or outside the classroom, will be divulged by his or her professors beyond the walls of the college community. If students anticipated that anything they said or wrote might be disclosed, they might not feel free to express their thoughts and ideas, and the critical inquiry, probing, and investigation essential to a free academy, might well be impaired.

The following standards are recommended as general guidelines: When questioned directly by representatives of government agencies or by prospective employers of any kind, public or private, or by investigative agencies or other persons, or indirectly by the institution's administrative officers in behalf of such agencies, a teacher may safely answer questions which he or she finds clearly connected with the student's competence and fitness for the job. There is always the chance, however, that even questions of this kind will inadvertently cause the teacher to violate academic privacy. Questions and answers in written form make it easier to avoid pitfalls, but the teacher's alertness is always essential. Ordinarily, questions relating to the student's academic performance as, for example, the ability to write clearly, to solve problems, to reason well, to direct projects, pose no threat to educational privacy. But questions relating to students' loyalties and patriotism, their political, religious, moral or social beliefs and attitudes, their general outlook, their private life may, if answered, violate the student's academic freedom and jeopardize the student-teacher relationship.

As a safeguard against the danger of placing the student in an unfavorable light with government agencies or employers of any category, teachers may preface each questionnaire with a brief *pro forma* statement that the academic policy to which they subscribe makes it inadvisable to answer certain types of questions about any or all students. Once this academic policy becomes widespread, presumptive inferences about individual students will no longer be made by employers.

Even when students request their teachers to disclose information other than relating to their academic performance because they think it would be advantageous—such disclosure should not be made since disclosure in individual cases would raise doubts about students who had made no such request. A satisfactory principle, therefore, would foreclose disclosure in all cases.

Faculty senates or other representative faculty bodies, it is hoped, will take cognizance of the teacher-disclosure problem, and recommend action which will leave inviolate the teacher-student relationship, and protect the privacy of the student. [Board Minutes, February 14-15, 1976.]

***

(b) The ACLU recommends that universities cease, on their own, to make available to Selective Service any information on grades and class rank. This is within the university's right to make decisions affecting the academic process, regardless of Selective Service regulations. The Union believes that academic values are perverted by tying military deferment to student grades and class rank. In such circumstances, grades take on a life and death significance which can only impair the whole educational enterprise. Selection of easy courses and institutions by students to maintain high class rank and thus assure military exemption further vitiates the academic process.

When an institution of higher learning decides as a matter of educational policy to cease calculating class standing, or to calculate standing but not report such data to the Selective Service, this does not constitute an infringement of a student's civil liberties.

When an institution follows a policy of compiling class standing for Selective Service purposes, as well as for academic purposes, a student's record should be made available to draft boards only at the request of the student.

If an institution has a known policy of grading, either written or implicit in the terms of employment, and if a teacher decides on his or her own not to submit grades, such action is not a matter of civil liberties concern. A teacher at a college or university is under an obligation to fulfill his or her responsibility to the university. Although a teacher's action in refusing to submit grades may be based on moral grounds and is analogous to an act of civil disobedience, it would not lessen the university's authority to make and enforce its own regulations. [Board Minutes, February 27, 1967, April 6, 1967; News Release, May 15, 1967.]

***

(c) No record, including that of conviction in a court of law, should be noted in a student's file unless there is a demonstrable need for it which is reasonably related to the basic purposes and necessities of the university.[1] Relevant records, such as academic, disciplinary, medical and psychiatric, should be maintained in separate files. Disciplinary records should be destroyed upon graduation.

No mention should be made in any university record of a student's religious or political beliefs or association or of the student's race or sex.[2]

Access to student records should be confined to authorized university personnel who require access in connection with the performance of their duties. All persons having access to student records should be instructed that the information contained therein must be kept confidential, and should be required to sign and date their adherence to this procedure.

Particular safeguards should be established with respect to medical (in-

[1] In October 1966, the United States Civil Service Commission dropped all inquiries concerning arrest from its federal employment application forms, stating that such queries "infringed the spirit of due process and was particularly hurtful to those citizens who were arrested not for committing ordinary crimes, but as reprisal for exercising First Amendment rights of speech and association in civil right demonstrations."

[2] We include race and sex in this list because we have in mind the situation in which an individual suffers discrimination (in admissions, financial aid consideration, grading, housing assignment, etc.) because his or her race or sex is indicated in university records. However, race and sex can be included in records relating to affirmative action programs in accordance with ACLU policies on affirmative action and collection of race information where a social utility is served.

cluding psychiatric) records. Such records should be subject to the same rules of confidentiality as apply for non-students and should not be construed to be "student records" for purposes of this section.

Persons outside the university should not have access to student academic records without the students' written permission, or to any other records, except in response to a constitutionally valid subpoena.[1] The institution should not itself be the sole agency for placing an individual in legal jeopardy by turning over information in response to a subpoena. Students whose records are subpoenaed should be immediately informed of the fact. [Board Minutes, February 14-15, 1976.]

POLICY UNDER REVIEW.

***

Further Information (not policy)

The 1974 Family Educational Rights and Privacy Act allows students and their parents access to school records, to contest the accuracy or propriety of entries, and to exercise some control over the dissemination of information from school files.

The Act applies to any "educational agency or institution" which receives federal funds administered through the Office of Education. This encompasses all public institutions and many private ones.

The rights accorded by the Act apply to present and former students. For students under age 18, the rights are exercised by their parents. "Eligible students," those age 18 and over, exercise their rights directly. The ACLU is disappointed by the failure to extend coverage to rejected applicants to schools. Without the right to inspect the records and letters of recommendation submitted with applications, unsuccessful applicants may never know why they were not admitted.

Among the documents exempted from the coverage of the Act are confidential letters of recommendation for post-secondary students filed prior to January 1, 1975. The ACLU opposes this exception because such letters are particularly important to students and contain precisely the kind of information which can be of greatest harm to students in seeking additional education, funds, or employment. The ACLU also opposes the statutory waiver provision affecting letters of recommendation on the grounds that waiver is always to an individual, but an explicit statutory provision might encourage institutions to extract such waivers as a condition of providing recommendations.

The Act also requires, subject to exceptions, consent before student records are released to outside parties.

---

[1] The term "constitutionally valid subpoena" is used to exclude subpoenas based on political investigation or other situations which, in the opinion of the Union, are unconstitutional.

C.I.A. and the Academic Community

(a) *Secret Research*

Secret research, consultation or other activities by academics for the C.I.A. should be subject to the same restraints applicable to any other secret work by academics. In this context, the ACLU reaffirms the policy on the University and Contract Research[1] as applied to matters involving the C.I.A.

Though academics may do work for the C.I.A., the *fact* of their doing such work must not be kept secret from their research subjects or from any members of the college community. The existence of a C.I.A. connection may well affect the kind of communications colleagues and students may make, and secrecy of employment with the C.I.A. necessarily corrodes the open atmosphere academic life requires to flourish.

***

(b) *Library Research*

A major part of the C.I.A.'s work involves library research and analyses of foreign and international politics and economic development using open sources of information. Academics engaging in such work raise no special problems unless they violate other university rules barring external part-time employment.

***

(c) *Recruitment*

College personnel who serve as C.I.A. recruiters of other university personnel should so identify themselves. Such identification should be made to the college or university to give notice to all concerned. At a minimum, this would require C.I.A. recruiters to register with the placement office. Further steps will be necessary to bring this information to all members of the college community, but the particular means for such identification should be developed by each individual institution.

---

[1] This policy states:

"Free and open inquiry and unhindered circulation of ideas are fundamental aspects of academic freedom. Externally funded and controlled research may divert the basic interest of the university as a free and open academic community and hence should be curtailed as an intrusion into academic freedom. Therefore, universities should not accept grants, or enter agreements for the support of instruction or research, which confer upon any external party, public or private, power to censor, to delay, or to exercise effective veto on either the contents of instruction or the dissemination of results and conclusions arising from instruction or research.

"Any work not open to critical professional judgment should not be used as a criterion for evaluation toward promotion, tenure or degree. Participation in such work should be separate from the usual instructional research and governance responsibilities.

"The university should enter no contract and accept no grant that involves the loyalty or security clearance of any person involved in the project.

"While the points above should be binding on the university as a corporate entity, faculty members must judge the validity and propriety of any arrangements that they may enter into with outside agencies in their capacity as individuals."

Names of individuals should not be supplied to the C.I.A. without the consent of the individual involved and then only through regular on-campus channels. Investigations of potential recruits should not be undertaken without their consent. College and university officials should insist that, if the C.I.A. does not hire the person investigated, the data developed in the investigation should be destroyed.

***

(d) *Reporting*
To preserve freedom of expression, faculty, students, administrators and other college personnel should not report to the C.I.A. the views or activities of fellow members of the academic community. With respect to students, there is an element of entrapment involved since they normally are encouraged to express themselves freely and openly.

***

(e) *Travel Abroad*
Academics who travel abroad are sometimes asked before they leave to gather information or to report back information to the C.I.A. Such reporting should be prohibited because it impairs the credibility of American scholars generally and violates the cardinal rules of openness and independence in scholarly research.

***

(f) *Guidelines*
No one should retroactively be considered to have violated his or her obligations as a teacher or scholar because of association with the C.I.A., overt or covert, before the adoption of professional, ethical guidelines by the university community. Of course, violation of any pre-existing professional norm, such as publication in one's name of material prepared by the C.I.A., may be the basis of disciplinary or other negative action affecting the individual. [Board Minutes, June 18-19, 1977.]

Policy #64

Academic Freedom and Scientific Research
Fundamental to the nature of scientific inquiry is the requirement that its views be open to critical assessment by appeal to independently validated evidence and rational argument freely disseminated to all persons. Freedom of inquiry in the pursuit of scientific knowledge is thus closely allied to freedom of speech and publication as well as to the traditional academic pursuit, articulation and dissemination of knowledge in general. However controversial their views and however unsettling they may be to accepted popular beliefs or to opposing scientific positions, scientists, as do researchers and scholars in general, have the

right to hold, propound, teach and publish their views unhampered by any but the most weighty considerations which would justify limitation on free speech as such. [Board Minutes, December 3-4, 1977.] (See policy on Teachers' Freedom and Responsibility and Due Process in Higher Education, first paragraph.)

Policy #67

College Student's Civil Liberties

(a) *The Student as a Member of the Academic Community*
The student's freedom to learn is a complement of the faculty member's freedom to teach. An academic community dedicated to its ideals will safeguard the one as vigorously as it does the other.

1) Admissions policies should be clearly defined, publicly stated, and uniformly administered to assure proper consideration for all applicants. Admission should not be denied on the basis of ethnic origin, race, religion, political belief or affiliation, sexual orientation, sex or any other basis incompatible with principles of equal opportunity. To achieve genuine equality of educational opportunity for members of disadvantaged groups, colleges should apply different standards and methods of evaluating applicants with such backgrounds, as long as these standards and methods are reasonably designed to increase the opportunity of these educationally deprived students. Massive compensatory programs for educationally deprived students should be simultaneously instituted. (See also policy on Employment.)

Students who chose imprisonment or exile as an alternative to military service should be eligible on release, or return to the U.S., for admission or readmission without prejudice to opportunities for financial aid.

2) Free and open discussion, speculation and investigation are basic to academic freedom. Students as well as teachers should be free to present their own opinions and findings. Teachers should evaluate student performance with scrupulous adherence to professional standards and without prejudice for the expression of views that may be controversial or unorthodox.

Television cameras, tape recorders and similar devices are being used with increasing frequency for educational purposes in colleges and universities. The use of such equipment in classrooms, in an ethical manner and for legitimate educational purposes, is not to be criticized. Caution must be exercised, however, to prevent the misuse of sight and sound recordings where they are likely to inhibit free and open discussion by teacher and student. Persons wishing to use tape recorders for the purpose of recording class lectures and/or discussions should do so only with the explicit knowledge and consent of the teacher and participants, and then only for that purpose. A faculty-student committee should establish guidelines for the use of electronic recording devices and for the disposition of records which are made.

***

(b) *The Student's Role in the Formulation of Academic Policy*

Colleges and universities should take whatever steps are necessary to enable student representatives to participate in an effective capacity with the faculty and administration in determining at every level, beginning with the departmental, such basic educational policies as course offerings and curriculum; the manner of grading; class size; standards for evaluating the performance of faculty members; and the relative allocation of the institution's resources among its various educational programs. Determination of what constitutes participation in an effective capacity in specific areas of decision-making may be assessed by individual institutions in accordance with reasonable standards. Student participation in some areas may be solely advisory, while in other areas, a voting role would be appropriate.

1) Operational funds should be supplied by the students themselves or the college administration. No student government, nor its national affiliate, should be covertly subsidized by any governmental agency. Students, through their duly elected representatives, should distribute available funds.

2) Students should be free, without restraint by either the college administration or the student government, to organize and join campus clubs or associations for educational, political, social, religious or cultural purposes. No such organization should discriminate on grounds of race, religion, color or national origin. The administration should not discriminate against a student because of membership in any campus organization.

The guidelines in this section apply to student organizations that seek official university recognition, subsidy, or free use of university facilities. They do not necessarily apply to off-campus organizations or those which do not have these privileges.

3) A procedure for official recognition of student organizations may be established by the student government. The group applying for recognition may be required only to submit the names of its officers and, if considered advisable, an affidavit that the organization is composed of students and stating their number if related to funding. The names of officers should not be disclosed without the consent of the individuals involved. The fact of affiliation with an extramural association should not, in itself, bar a group from recognition, but disclosure of such fact may be required.

Meeting rooms and other campus facilities should be made available to student organizations on a non-discriminatory basis as far as their primary use for educational purposes permits. Bulletin boards should be provided for the use of student organizations; school-wide circulation of all notices and leaflets should be permitted.

No student organization should be required to have a faculty adviser, but if it wishes one, it should be free to choose one for itself. An adviser should consult with and counsel the organization but should have no authority or responsibility to regulate or control its activities.

5) Students should have the right to assemble, to select speakers and guests, and to discuss issues of their choice. It should be clear to the public that an invitation to a speaker does not imply approval of the speaker's views by either the student group or the college administration. Students should enjoy the same right as other citizens to hear different points of view and draw their own conclusions. When a student group wishes to hear a controversial or socially unpopular speaker, the college should not require that a spokesman for an opposing viewpoint be scheduled either simultaneously or on a subsequent occasion. The college should seek to protect the safety of students and speakers who are unpopular and should do everything in their power to allow such speakers the right to be heard.

6) All student publications—college newspapers, literary and humor magazines, academic periodicals and yearbooks—should enjoy full freedom of the press, and not be restricted by either the administration or the student government. This should be the practice even though most college publications, except for the relatively few university dailies which are financially autonomous, are dependent on the administration's favor for the use of campus facilities, and are subsidized either directly or indirectly by a tax on student funds. Student initiation of competing publications should not be discouraged.

Where there is a single college newspaper supported from student fees or other resources of the college, it should impartially cover news and should serve as a forum for opposing views on controversial issues. It may also be expected to deal in news columns and editorials with the political and social issues that are relevant to the concerns of the students as citizens of the larger community. Neither the faculty, administration, board of trustees nor legislature should be immune from criticism.

Wherever plausible a student newspaper should be financially and physically separate from the college, existing as a legally independent corporation. The college would then be absolved from legal liability for the publication and bear no direct responsibility to the community for the views expressed. In those cases where college papers do not enjoy financial independence, no representative of the college should exercise veto power in the absence of a specific finding of potential libel as determined by an impartial legal authority. In no case, however, should the decision of the editor or editors be challenged or overruled simply because of pressure from alumni, the board of trustees, the state legislature, the college administration or the student government.

Where there is a college publications board, it should be composed of at least a majority of students selected by the student government or council, or by some other democratic method. Should the board, or in case the paper has no board, an *ad hoc* committee selected by the faculty and student government, maintain that the editor has been guilty of deliberate malice or deliberate distortion, the validity of this charge should be determined through due process.

7) Campus radio and television stations should enjoy and exercise the same editorial freedom as the college press. Stations whose signals go beyond the campus operate under a license granted by the Federal Communications Commission and, therefore, must conform to the applicable regulations of the Commission.

The same freedom from censorship enjoyed by other communications media should be extended to on-campus artistic presentations, such as film festivals, etc.

***

(c) *The Ethics of Scholarship*

So that students may become fully aware of the ethics of scholarship, the faculty should draw up a clear statement as to what constitutes plagiarism or improper use of another's work, setting forth principles the students will understand and respect. This should be made available to students. Any student charged with such a violation should be accorded a due process hearing.

***

(d) *Extracurricular Activities*

Students receive their college education not only in the classroom but also in out-of-class activities which they themselves organize through their association with fellow students, the student press, student organizations and in other ways. It is vital, therefore, that their freedom as campus citizens be respected and ensured.

Student government in the past has had as one of its chief functions the regulation of student-sponsored activities, organizations, publications, etc. In exercising this function, no student government should be permitted to allocate resources so as to bar or intimidate any campus organization or publication nor make regulations which violate basic principles of academic freedom and civil liberties.

Delegates to the student government should be elected by democratic process by the student body and should not represent merely clubs or organizations. Designation of officers, committees, and boards should also be by democratic process, should be non-discriminatory, and should not be subject either to administrative or faculty approval. Any enrolled student should be eligible for election to student office. In universities, graduate students should be afforded the opportunity to participate in student government.

***

(e) *Students' Political Freedom*

American college students possess the same right to freedom of speech, assembly and association as do other residents of the United States. They are also subject to the same obligations and responsibilities as persons who are not members of the academic communities.

1) Students should be free through organized action on campus to register their political views or their disapprobation of university policies, but within peaceful limits. The use of force on a college campus—whether by students, the campus police, or outside police called in by the administration—is always to be regretted. Outside police should not be summoned to a campus to deal with internal problems, unless essential and unless all other techniques have clearly failed.

2) Failure of communication among administration, faculty and students has been a recurrent cause of campus crises. Prompt consultation by the administration with faculty and student spokesmen may serve to prevent potentially disastrous confrontations which disrupt the orderly processes of the institution.

Picketing, demonstrations, sit-ins, or student strikes, provided they are conducted in an orderly and non-obstructive manner are legitimate activities whether they are instigated by events outside the campus or directed against the college administration, and should not be prohibited, nor should students be penalized for engaging in them. Demonstrators or distributors of pamphlets, however, have no right to deprive others of the opportunity to speak or be heard; take hostages; physically obstruct the movement of others; or otherwise disrupt the educational or institutional processes in a way that interferes with the safety or freedom of others.

Students should be free, and no special permission should be required, to distribute pamphlets or collect names for petitions concerned with campus or off-campus issues. Colleges may not deny financial aid or impose lower grades so as to penalize students for political activity.

Regulations governing demonstrations should be made by a committee of administrators, representative faculty, and democratically selected students. The regulations should be drawn so as to protect the students' First Amendment rights to the fullest extent possible and, at the same time, ensure against disruption of the academic process as, for example, by the use of high volume loudspeakers or other techniques which curtail the freedom of others.

Student participation in off-campus activities such as peace marches, civil rights demonstrations, draft protests, picketing, boycotts, political campaigns, public rallies, non-campus publications and acts of civil disobedience is not the legitimate concern of the college or university.

Students, like teachers, have the right to identify themselves as members of a particular academic community. But they also have the moral obligation not to misrepresent the views of others in their academic community.

***

(f) *Personal Freedom*

1) College students should be free to organize their personal lives and determine their private behavior free from institutional interference. In the past many colleges, with the approval of parents and the acquiescence of students,

have played the role of surrogate parents. This function is now being strongly challenged. An increasing number of institutions today recognize that students, as part of the maturing process, must be permitted to assume responsibility for their private lives—even if, in some instances, their philosophies or conduct are at variance with traditional standards.

The college community should not regard itself as the arbiter of personal behavior or morals, as long as the conduct does not interfere with the rights of others. Regulation is appropriate only if necessary to protect the health, safety, and academic pursuits of members of the academic community.

2) Although on-campus living is often regarded as an important part of the total educational experience, it should not be made compulsory for parietal reasons. Where parietal regulations are invoked they should apply without distinction as to sex or class year.

Medical and health facilities should not deny services appropriate to the needs of either sex.

Dress and grooming are modes of personal expression and taste which should be left to the individual except for reasonable requirements related to health and safety (such as wearing proper attire while participating in gym activities), and except for ceremonial occasions the nature of which requires particular dress or grooming.

If a student is pregnant she should be free to decide for herself when to take leave of her studies. A university should treat a possible extended absence resulting from pregnancy like any other medical problem.

Students' lockers should not be opened, or their rooms searched, without their consent except in conformity with the intent of the Fourth Amendment which requires that a warrant first be obtained on a showing of probable cause, supported by oath or affirmation, and particularly describing the things to be seized.

***

(g) *Regulations and Disciplinary Procedures*

1) Regulations governing student conduct should be in harmony with and essential to the fulfillment of the college's educational objectives. Students should participate fully and effectively in formulating and adjudicating college regulations governing student conduct. Reasonable procedures should be established and followed in enforcing discipline.

Regulations should be clear and unambiguous. Phrases such as "conduct unbecoming a student," or "actions against the best interests of the college," should be avoided because they allow too much latitude for interpretation.

The range of penalties for the violation of regulations should be clearly specified. Rules which automatically impose very severe penalties should be avoided.

Regulations should be published and circulated to the entire academic community.

Minor infractions of college regulations, penalized by small fines or reprimands which do not become part of a student's permanent record, may be handled summarily by the appropriate administrative, faculty or student officer. However, the student should have the right to appeal.

In the case of infractions of college regulations which may lead to more serious penalties, such as suspension, expulsion, or notation on a student's permanent record, the student is entitled to formal procedures in order to prevent a miscarriage of justice.[1]

These procedures should include a formal hearing by a student-faculty or a student judicial committee. No member of the hearing committee who is involved in the particular case should sit in judgment.

Prior to the hearing the student should be: 1) advised in writing of the charges against him, including a summary of the evidence upon which the charges are based; 2) advised that he is entitled to be represented and advised at all times during the course of the proceedings by a person of his own choosing, including outside counsel; 3) advised of the procedures to be followed at the hearing.

At the hearing, the student (or his/her representative) and the member of the academic community bringing charges (or his/her representative) should each have the right to testify, although the student should not be compelled to do so, and each should have the right to examine and cross-examine witnesses and to present documentary and other evidence in support of respective contentions. The college administration should make available to the student such authority as it may possess to require the presence of witnesses and the production of documents at the hearing. A full record should be taken at the hearing and it should be made available in identical form to the hearing panel, the administration and the student. After the hearing is closed, the panel should adjudicate the matter before it with reasonable promptness and submit its finding and conclusions in writing. Copies thereof should be made available in identical form, and at the same time, to the administration and the student. The cost should be met by the institution.

After completion of summary or formal proceedings, the right of appeal should be permitted only to the student. On appeal, the decision of the hearing Board should be affirmed, modified or reversed but the penalty, if any, not increased.

A college should not impose sanctions for the sole reason that a student is or has been involved in criminal proceedings.

A student charged with or convicted of a crime should not be subject to academic sanctions by the college for the same conduct unless the offense is of such a nature that the institution needs to impose its own sanction upon the

---

[1] A student may not be suspended except in exceptional circumstances involving danger to health, safety or disruption of the educational process. Within twenty-four hours of suspension, or wherever possible prior to such action, the student should be given a written statement explaining why the suspension could not await a hearing.

student for the protection of other students or to safeguard the academic process. Where there is a possibility that testimony and other evidence at a college hearing would be subject to disclosure by way of subpoena in a subsequent court proceeding, college disciplinary hearings should be postponed to safeguard the student's right to a fair determination in the criminal proceeding.

Colleges should be especially scrupulous to avoid further sanctions attendant upon criminal convictions for conduct that should have been entitled to protection of the First Amendment even if the student's First Amendment claim was not recognized by the Court which convicted him or her, and for conduct which, while validly punishable, was a peaceable act of social, political or religious protest that did not threaten the academic process.

2) Police presence on the campus is detrimental to the educational mission of the university and should be avoided if at all possible. In those last-resort situations, where all efforts to resolve campus disorders internally have failed, the institution may have to invite police to the campus to maintain or restore public order.

Guidelines and procedures for summoning off-campus law enforcement authorities should be established by a committee representing the administration, faculty and students. This committee should also determine the duties and prerogatives of campus security officers.

The proper function of law officers in crime detection cannot be impeded. Members of the academic community, however, should not function surreptitiously on campus as agents for law enforcement authorities. Such action is harmful to the climate of free association essential to a college community. Similarly, the university should not sanction those surreptitious or undercover activities of police officers—such as masquerading as teachers or students—which can be expected to exercise a chilling effect on free speech.

(See also policy on the CIA and the Academic Community and Government Surveillance.)

***

(h) *Students and the Military*

1) Colleges have an educational function to perform and should not become an adjunct of the military. Such a development would constitute a threat to their survival as centers of critical inquiry.

Information concerning the student's enrollment and standing should be submitted to Selective Service by the college only at the request of the student.[1]

2) Unless a college bars all occupational recruitment of students, the Army,

---

[1] In a letter to the ACLU, dated December 2, 1968, Deputy Director of Selective Service, Daniel O. Omer, stated: "The responsibility for keeping a selective service board informed regarding the current student status of a registrant is upon the registrant himself and not upon the college."

Navy and Air Force should be allowed the same campus facilities as other government agencies and private corporations.[1]

3) On campuses where Reserve Officer Training Corps programs exist, student enrollment should be on a voluntary basis. Academic credit should be granted only for those ROTC courses which are acceptable to and under the control of the regular faculty. ROTC instructors should not hold academic rank unless they are members of an academic department subject to the regular procedures of appointment and removal. All ROTC programs should abide by campus rules and regulations and should fully observe ACLU policies regarding the maintenance of records which relate or refer to social, religious, or political views or associations of the student. [Board Minutes, February 14-15, 1976.] (See policy on ROTC.)

***

Further Information (not policy)

In *Healy v. James* (1972), the Supreme Court struck down a state college's denial of official recognition to a local chapter of the Students for a Democratic Society. The Court commented that precedents "leave no room for the view that . . . First Amendment protections should apply with less force on college campuses than in the community at large."

In 1973, a non-resident state university student, expelled for distributing an allegedly obscene and indecent underground newspaper, and thus violating a university by-law prohibiting "indecent conduct or speech," contended that her expulsion was based on protected First Amendment activities. The Supreme Court, in *Papish v. Board of Curators of the University of Missouri* (1973), required that the student be reinstated. It held that the university's regulation of the content of speech was not beyond the purview of the First Amendment but that neither the article nor the cartoon in question could be labeled obscene and thus unprotected speech.

Policy #70

Selection of School and Library Materials and Pressure Group Attacks

(a) *Introduction*

One of the objectives of universal free public education is to develop in children the intellectual capacities required for the effective exercise of the

---

[1] Since on-campus recruitment is essentially a service to students and not central to the educational purposes of the university, colleges may prohibit all recruitment as a matter of institutional policy. But if outside recruitment is allowed, the ACLU believes it should be on a non-discriminatory basis and in accordance with established policies and procedures. Selective exclusions, arising primarily from a political controversy, that deny students access to particular recruiters are discriminatory in their applications and suggest a possible infringement of the spirit of the equal protection clause of the Constitution.

rights and duties of citizenship. Experience demonstrates that this is best accomplished in an atmosphere of free inquiry and discussion which is, in turn, supported by effective selection and use of instructional materials. This policy statement attempts to establish the rights and responsibilities of all the participants in this essential process and provide standards and procedures for selecting textbook and library materials consistent with the developments as citizens in a free society. [Board Minutes, June 18-19, 1977.]

***

(b) *General Guidelines*

1) Instructional materials, including *inter alia texts*, books, films, magazines, and newspapers, should make available to students in their classes and in school libraries, a wide range of ideas, and diversity of political viewpoints. Such diversity is required by the constitutional guarantee of free speech, free press, and equal protection. Material should never be excluded or removed simply because it expresses unpopular, or controversial views, or because it coincides with particular religious views, provided that texts or materials which give a particular religious explanation of any subject may not be used in the public schools in such a context as to further or inculcate religion. The requirement of diversity, however, does not mandate a presentation of any particular point of view or theory unless necessary to a fair and balanced presentation of the subject. [Board Minutes, June 18-19, 1977.]

2) At times, implementation of these objectives will induce conscientious teachers, librarians, and other professionals entrusted with the task of making or recommending choices of instructional materials, to choose materials which may be characterized as "un-American," "communistic," "obscene" or "irreverent," by some community individuals or groups, including Board of Education members. This may lead to attempts to eliminate these materials to punish teachers and librarians for their use, and to substitute other materials more congenial to certain political and religious beliefs. [Board Minutes, September 24-25, 1977.]

3) The ACLU is strongly committed to the principle of free inquiry and diversity at all educational levels. Therefore, the ACLU will employ all appropriate means to protect school systems, teachers, librarians, and students attempting to implement these principles of diversity from attacks by groups espousing a narrower view of the educational process. But the ACLU also recognizes the right of parents and students to some measure of protection from compulsory use of instructional materials which they believe assault religious and moral beliefs. [Board Minutes, June 18-19, 1977.]

4) School boards, or other bodies with the ultimate statutory authority to approve instructional materials, should be elected or appointed by procedures that permit meaningful public participation. [Board Minutes, September 24-25, 1977.]

***

(c) *Classroom Instructional Materials*

1) Selection of classroom instructional materials is primarily the responsibility of professional educators. But school boards, parents, students, and the community are entitled to participate in the process.

2) a) The best method for selecting teaching materials is to give final authority to teachers to make selections on the basis of their professional competence in consultation with supervisors and within guidelines established by school boards. Such guidelines should conform to the general principles provided herein. Recommendations from students, parents, and citizens should be considered. Teachers should respect the right of students to freedom of inquiry and to access to materials offering a variety of views on controversial issues. In making their selections, teachers may properly take into account the degree of maturity of the students as well as the educational effectiveness of instructional materials. Their responsibility also includes review and replacement of outdated materials.

b) States and communities may choose to require school boards to give final approval to selections after consultation with educators and the community. School boards, however, may not exercise such authority so as to implement particular viewpoints on debatable economic, social, political, moral, and literary issues.

***

(d) *Libraries*

1) Library materials should be selected by librarians, taking into account recommendations from teachers, members of the community, students, and parents, and within guidelines established by school boards. Such guidelines should conform to the general principles provided herein. Library materials should present the multiple realities of a pluralistic society including fiction and non-fiction which portray the many facets of life and provide a full airing of controversial issues. School board members, individually or as a body, may not ban or remove materials from libraries.

2) In addition to the obligation to include a wide range of ideas and interpretations in the materials in the school library, the library also has an affirmative duty to provide access to materials to students. The library should not refuse access to books and other materials to students on the grounds of a student's age, sex, race, ethnic group, or religion, and should not restrict access because of the alleged inappropriateness of the subject matter.

***

(e) *Complaint Procedures*

Criticism of books and materials selected and advocacy of additional material is an essential free speech right of students, parents, faculty, and the community. A written, clearly defined method should be adopted by each school district for handling suggestions and complaints. This should include written statements of proposals or objections, identification of the material, open, well-publicized hearings, review by educators and librarians and other resource persons, and decisions made within a reasonable period of time. Objection to the particular language or viewpoint of material cannot be justification for the exclusion of classroom or library material. Material objected to may not be withdrawn from use while the objection is being reviewed. [Board Minutes, June 18-19, 1977.]

(See also policy on Private Pressure Groups.)

***

Further Information (not policy)

In *President's Council, District 65 v. Community School Board, No. 25* (1972), the United States Court of Appeals for the Second Circuit found no violation of the First Amendment when a local school board voted to require the removal of a particular book from junior high school libraries. The Court noted that the book, *Down these Mean Streets* by Piri Thomas, concerning the life of a young person in Spanish Harlem, could remain in the libraries that already had it. Moreover, the book would be made available on loan to any parent who could then offer it to his or her child. The court found no "curtailment of speech or thought." Rather, it viewed the Board's action as a simple matter of shelving and unshelving library books and for that reason lacking constitutional dimension. However, in *Minarcini v. Strongsville City School District* (1976), the United Court of Appeals for the Sixth Circuit held that where the school board did not explain its actions in removing particular books from the public school library, and there was evidence that the board was censoring school library books that it found distasteful, the removal of these books was found to violate the First Amendment as an unconstitutional curtailment of speech and thought.

Policy #93

Governmental Use of Religious Organizations for Overseas Relief Programs

Extensive administrative participation by religious agencies in federal foreign aid programs as well as partial government financing for certain church-organized foreign aid programs clearly present a challenge to the separation of church and state. Churches themselves may be beneficiaries as well as administrators of such programs, a situation which runs counter the ACLU's general policy on church-state relations. In their own activities churches may also be unduly restricted abroad by U.S. governmental policy as a result of participation in such programs. Therefore, the ACLU recommends the following policy:

1) Public benefits for the alleviation of extreme hardships of a compelling human nature, should, as a general rule, be channeled through secular organizations. Religious organizations should be utilized only temporarily and then only in situations where there exist no adequate secular or private non-religious organizations, and then only until the United States government can arrange public channels for distribution of public resources.

If religious organizations are utilized then:

a) All such arrangements should operate on a contract for specific services.

b) Public funds should cover only the costs arising from the secular services rendered under the contract.

c) All contracts should have specific terminal dates.

d) All contracts should explicitly prohibit proselytism activities while the church institutions are engaged in the distribution of public benefits.

2) No religious test of membership, practice or belief should be required of any persons seeking, receiving or delivering public benefits, services or employment in any publicly financed program. [Board Minutes, April 10-11, 1976.]

Policy #94

Kidnapping Young People from Religious Groups

The ACLU opposes the use of mental incompetency proceedings, conservatorships, temporary guardianships, or denial of government protection as a method of depriving people, at least with respect to those who have attained the age of majority, of the free exercise of religion.

Modes of religious proselytizing or persuasion for a continued adherence that do not employ physical coercion or threat of same are protected by the free exercise of religion clause of the First Amendment against action through state laws or by state officials. The claim of free exercise may not be overcome by the contention that "brainwashing" or "mind control" has been used, in the absence of evidence that the above standards have been violated. [Board Minutes, March 5-6, 1977.]

Policy #108

Governmental Surveillance

General Policy

The ACLU opposes the use of undercover agents to infiltrate any private association as endangering the rights of speech, association and privacy. [Board Minutes, February 14-15, 1970.]

No official or employee of any government agency shall pose or act, or direct another person to pose or act, as a member or associate of a group for the purpose of political intelligence gathering. This prohibition should be enforced by civil remedies and criminal penalties. Political intelligence gathering is the practice of collecting, processing, storing and/or disseminating information concerning a person's or group's beliefs, thoughts, opinions or political associations and activities. [Board Minutes, September 24-25, 1977.]

The ACLU condemns the widespread and uncurbed use of police spies in organizations engaged in political activity because it violates the rights of freedom of speech and association protected by the First Amendment, the right to be free of unreasonable searches and seizures guaranteed by the Fourth Amendment, and the general right of privacy protected by the Bill of Rights. Historically, police agents have been one of the instruments used by governments to discourage or crush opposition to official policies.

The use of police spies offends the fundamental notion that citizens have the right to associate among themselves to achieve social or political objectives in which they believe without interference by the government. Thus, the introduction of government spies into such associations facilitates the collection of information which is none of the government's business. Since it is known that the police infiltrate some controversial organizations, it may well be assumed by the public that they infiltrate all controversial organizations. Consequently, membership in all such organizations is discouraged and constitutionally protected activity is interfered with.

Furthermore, experience shows that government spies do not always limit their activity to the gathering of information. Such agents have also acted as provocateurs who encourage illegal acts in order to discredit publicly controversial organizations. Such agents have also been known to encourage illegal acts in order to entrap individual members in criminal acts.

The introduction of government agents into these associations also is illegal because it is the equivalent to the use of general warrants, forbidden by the Fourth Amendment. That Amendment requires that a warrant can be issued only when there is probable cause to believe that a crime has been committed and the warrant must particularly describe the place to be searched and the things to be seized. But government spies, like government wiretaps, know no such limitations. Everything that is said and everything that is done over an unlimited period of time comes into the hands of the government, no matter how private, how unconnected with a legitimate state interest.

It is well known that the information gathered by government agents who infiltrate entirely lawful organizations is collected by a variety of government agencies and often used to the disadvantage of private individuals. This raw information has often been used to deny individuals government employment or other benefits and has also been used unlawfully by congressional committees bent only on discrediting individuals and organizations which have no effective remedy against the use and circulation of this information on the floor of the Congress.

The ACLU will in appropriate circumstances undertake litigation on behalf of an organization which is the victim of police infiltration. The ACLU also will take steps to determine and publicize the extent and nature of police infiltration of political organizations. The ACLU also will support legislation, at every level of government, designed to achieve the objectives set forth in this statement. Finally, the ACLU will use its facilities to discourage officials at every level of government from using or condoning the use of police spies to collect information about participants in political activity. [Board Minutes, February 14-15, 1970.]

Use of Informers in Groups Engaging in Criminal Activity

The ACLU takes the position that informers[1] may be employed only in organizations that may engage or may be planning to engage in the commission of serious criminal acts. These crimes must be limited to those commonly known as major crimes, such as kidnapping, murder and bombing, as such acts either deprive or adversely affect the civil rights and liberties of others. The permissible activities of informers in such organizations must be curtailed, however, because of the very real threat that they pose to the exercise of the First Amendment rights to peaceable assembly, association, free speech and privacy.

Before an informer may be used in such an organization, there must be a showing of probable cause narrowly construed that members of the organization were involved in the commission of the criminal act or were planning to commit a criminal act. In addition, a warrant must be obtained from a judge which must specify the specific section of the organization to be investigated, and which must limit the length of time that the warrant will be valid. Applications for extensions of the warrant must be examined by the same judge who originally granted the warrant to determine whether and for how long the warrant may be extended. If a warrant is renewed, a limit must be placed on the number of times that such extensions may be granted. Any such warrant shall have time limitations, renewal limitations and reporting requirements no less stringent than those required in the Safe Streets Act.

Because the First Amendment plays a crucial role in the democratic process, the ACLU takes the position that law enforcement agencies which fail to observe the civil liberties mandate to be as minimally intrusive as possible stand liable for violation of these constitutionally protected rights. The use of informers as agents provocateurs is constitutionally impermissible. The use of informers to collect information on the purely political activities or private lives of members of such organizations is constitutionally impermissible. [Board Minutes, December 3-4, 1977.]

Military Surveillance

The surveillance of lawful civilian political activity by the military branch of the government is a violation of the First Amendment and beyond the lawful authority of the Armed Forces.

---

[1] An informer is deemed to include any person secretly inserted into, recruited from, maintained or facilitated in an organization by a governmental agency to give information about alleged criminal activity in the organization. The term 'informer', as used in the policy statement, does not include the individual who voluntarily contacts, without any governmental participation as specified above, a governmental agency to supply it with information concerning criminal activity engaged in by members of the organization.

Military surveillance has included the indiscriminate collection, distribution, and storage of detailed information about the identities, actions, and beliefs of thousands of politically active, law-abiding individuals and organizations wholly unassociated with the Armed Forces; undercover operations by military agents within the civilian community; the maintenance of over a dozen regional and national record centers on political protests; and the distribution to military units and to federal agencies of hundreds of identification lists describing individuals and organizations who have objected to governmental policies and social conditions.

The ACLU condemns these activities as exceeding any legitimate military need or authority, as inhibiting political participation and debate, and as depriving dissenters of the rights of free speech and association, the right to petition the government for redress of grievances, and the right of privacy guaranteed by the First, Fourth, Fifth, and Ninth Amendments to the Constitution.

Intelligence activities by the military arm of the government bear especially close scrutiny by the courts. The continued supremacy of the civilian authorities over the military is fundamental to American government.

Governmental surveillance and maintenance of dossiers on persons who engage in protest against government policies and programs constitute a burden which may deter the more cautious and discreet from engaging in protest activity, or from expressing their opinions in the First Amendment context. The First Amendment is intended to allow freedom to criticize and change governmental policy where it deviates from its heritage or commitments. If the government can command silent obedience simply because of fear of speaking out, the people have lost their ultimate control over arbitrary governmental power. [ACLU brief, *Tatum v. Laird*, 1970.]

Special Governmental Practices

Certain federal, state, and local governmental agencies have made a practice of photographing, tape recording, and listing names and descriptions of persons attending meetings or lawful political demonstrations for the purpose of maintaining dossiers on such persons and the organizations sponsoring their activities. The ACLU condemns such surveillance and the maintenance of dossiers on persons and organizations engaged in activities protected by the First Amendment because of their inhibitory effect on the exercise of First Amendment rights.

The role of the police in preserving order at assemblies, meetings, and marches should be completely separate from the investigatory role of the police. When police maintain order at large public gatherings or are invited to smaller meetings where disruptive actions are expected, they should not engage in surveillance, either overt or covert, for the purpose of maintaining dossiers.

The ACLU advocates that all dossiers with respect to political association, expression of opinion or other exercises of constitutional rights of any persons should be destroyed.

Police regulations should set forth specific standards for obtaining and maintaining information on criminal activities. In addition, there should be provision for public challenge of police abuse of such standards. [Board Minutes, December 5-6, 1970.]

(See also policy on Civil Disobedience, on Picketing, on Controlling the Intelligence Agencies and on Demonstrations and College Students' Civil Liberties.)

***

Further Information (not policy)

Several recent Supreme Court cases have addressed matters concerning government surveillance. *United States v. United States District Court* (1972) involved the power of the President, acting through the Attorney General, to authorize electronic surveillance in internal security matters without prior judicial approval. A defendant charged with the bombing of a CIA office alleged that the government had obtained information against him as a result of electronic surveillance conducted without prior judicial approval. The government argued that the surveillance was legal as a reasonable exercise of the President's power to protect national security. The Supreme Court concluded that the government had not made out a sufficient case for its requested departure from the warrant requirement of the Fourth Amendment. The Court said that official surveillance, whether for the purpose of criminal investigation or ongoing intelligence gathering, risks infringement of constitutionally protected speech. The Court observed that security surveillances are especially sensitive due to the inherent vagueness of the concept of domestic security, the broad and continuing nature of intelligence gathering and the temptation to utilize such surveillance to oversee political dissent.

Laird v. Tatum (1972) involved a group of plaintiffs who alleged that their First Amendment rights were violated by surveillance of lawful civilian political activity allegedly carried on by the Department of the Army. The plaintiffs alleged that these surveillance activities had a "chilling effect" on their exercise of First Amendment rights. The Court said that a chilling effect could not arise merely from the knowledge that the government was engaged in certain surveillance activities or from the concomitant fear that, armed with the fruits of these activities, a government agency might take some action in the future detrimental to that individual.

In *Eastland v. United States Servicemens' Fund* (1974) a Senate subcommittee began investigating the USSF to determine if their anti-war activities were potentially harmful to the morale of the Armed Forces. The subcommittee subpoenaed a bank to produce all records concerning USSR's account, and USSF sought to enjoin the subpoena contending that its First Amendment rights would be violated if the names of its contributors were disclosed. The Supreme

Court held that the activities of the subcommittee, the individual Senators and the Chief Counsel were covered by the absolute protection of the Speech and Debate Clause of the Constitution. The Court said this clause immunized the subcommittee action from judicial scrutiny or interference.

Policy #109

Controlling the Intelligence Agencies

Control of our government's intelligence agencies demands an end to tolerance of "national security" as grounds for the slightest departure from the constitutional restraints which limit government conduct in other areas. Preservation of the Bill of Rights as a meaningful limitation on government power demands no less. Government secrecy must be drastically curtailed while restoring citizens' freedom from governmental scrutiny of and interference in their lives. To end that secrecy, limit government surveillance, and create effective enforcement mechanisms the following measures should be adopted:

(a) *Drastic Reduction of Secrecy*

1) Limit the authority of the Executive Branch to classify to three categories of information: technical details of weaponry, knowledge of which would be of benefit to another nation, technical details of tactical military operations in time of declared war, and defensive military contingency plans in response to attacks by foreign powers, but not including plans of surveillance in respect of domestic activity.

2) Create a mandatory exemption from classification of any information relating to United States activities in violation of United States laws.

3) Limit executive privilege to the "advice" privilege, guaranteeing Congressional access to all other information no matter what its classification. Congress would also have access to "advice" when it has probable cause to believe it contains evidence of criminal wrongdoing or violation of the limits Congress imposed by statute or resolution on intelligence activities.

4) Make absolute the right of Congress to release unilaterally information classified by the Executive Branch. Individual members of Congress cannot be restrained by classification procedures from releasing information which contains evidence of criminal wrongdoing or violations of the statutory limits to be imposed on intelligence activities.

5) Define proper roles for intelligence activities in public debate (see (b)). Make the budgets for the various intelligence agencies public.

6) Make it a crime for intelligence agency officials or senior non-elected policy makers willfully to deceive Congress or the public regarding activities which violate the criminal law or limits to be imposed on intelligence agencies.

7) Make it a criminal offense for a federal official whose duties are other than ministerial willfully to fail to report evidence of criminal conduct or conduct in violation of these limits to the Special Prosecutors (see (d)).

8) Protect "whistle blowers" in order to encourage revelation of activities which violate the criminal law or these limitations to Congress and to the public.

***

(b) *Public Determination of Agency's Activities*

1) Create legislative charters for each major agency, all provisions of which are to be publicly known. These would provide that all activities not specifically authorized therein are prohibited. The details would be required to be spelled out in agency regulations which are subject to public comment and Congressional control.

2) Limit the terms of agency heads. Also increase the independence of general counsels and require their written opinion on the legality of any operations which raise questions about compliance with any section of this policy.

3) Limit the CIA, under the new name of the Foreign Intelligence Agency, to collecting and evaluating foreign intelligence information. Abolish all covert and clandestine activity.

4) Prohibit the peacetime use of spies in the collection of foreign intelligence. Abolish clandestine organizations[1] for intelligence collection. Enact precisely drawn criminal sanctions against clandestine governmental relationships with citizens[2] and against the payments of public or private funds and other things of value, directly or indirectly, to citizens of our own and foreign nations for peacetime spying and espionage.

5) Restrict the FBI to criminal investigations by eliminating all COINTEL-PRO-type activity and all foreign and domestic intelligence investigations of groups or individuals unrelated to a specific criminal offense.

6) Limit the IRS to investigations of tax liability and tax crimes. The IRS' access to, or collection of, information on taxpayers' political views and activities should be barred.

7) Prohibit the National Security Agency from intercepting and recording international communications of Americans and resident aliens in the United States, whether via telecommunication, computer lines, or other means.

8) Prohibit the military from playing any role in civilian surveillance. No information on civilians and military personnel exercising constitutional rights should be collected. (See also policy on Governmental Surveillance.)

9) Establish a separate agency to conduct security clearance investigations for federal employees, judgeships and presidential appointees. Investigations

---

[1] A "clandestine organization" is one whose agents, officers, members, stockholders, or employees, or its activities, characteristics, functions, name, nature or salaries are secret.

[2] "Citizen" includes individuals and associations, corporations, firms, partnerships, and other organizations.

should not take place without the applicant's authorization. Files should be kept separate and limited to the purpose of the security investigation. Exceptions in the 1974 Privacy Act which deny people access to their files should be repealed.

10) Flatly prohibit exchange of information between agencies, except for evidence of espionage and other crimes which may be sent to the agency responsible for investigating or prosecuting them. Existing government files on First Amendment political activities should be destroyed.

***

(c) *Legislative Limits on Investigative Techniques*

1) Prohibit entirely wiretaps, tapping of telecommunications and burglaries. (See also policy on Privacy.)

2) Restrict mail openings, mail covers, inspection of bank records, and inspection of telephone records by requiring a warrant issued on probable cause to believe a crime has been committed. (See also policy on Mail Covers.)

3) Prohibit all domestic intelligence and political information-gathering. Only investigations of crimes which have been, are being, or are about to be committed may be conducted.

4) Prohibit the recording of and keeping files on those attending political meetings or engaging in other peaceful political activities. (See also policy on Governmental Surveillance.)

5) Make limitations public in regulations subject to public comment and Congressional control.

***

(d) *Enforcement*

1) Make it a criminal offense for an official knowingly to order the violation of the above restrictions on both the scope of the agency's activity and its techniques.

It should also be a separate criminal offense to fail to report violation of the restrictions described in a, b and c to the Special Prosecutor or to deceive Congress and the public about the same.

2) Create a permanent and independent Office of Special Prosecutor to police the intelligence community. The mandate should be limited to the investigation and prosecution of crimes committed by officials involved in this area. There should be time limits on the length of time the Special Prosecutor and his or her staff may serve. In addition the Office should have a mandate to initiate probes of other government agencies to find violations, as well as to prosecute those alleged violators brought to its attention. It should have access to all intelligence community files, and be empowered to use any information necessary for a successful prosecution of criminal offense. If the information is used, it must be given to the defendant.

3) Establish a wide-range of civil remedies for those whose rights have been violated by intelligence officials or organizations, patterned after those now available for victims of unauthorized wiretaps and violations of the Privacy Act.

Such a statute should eliminate the present jurisdictional amount of requirement; eliminate any need to prove actual damage or injury; declare certain practices to be injurious and provide liquidated damages for those aggrieved; provide recovery of attorneys' fees and costs; and disallow a "good faith" defense.

***

(e) *Congressional Oversight*

1) Create *separate* committees in each House with jurisdiction over authorization of funds for CIA, NSA, and FBI; legislative authority on entire range of intelligence activities; oversight of all agencies engaging in intelligence activities; a special mandate to oversee and legislate with respect to: (a) compliance with sharply curtailed classification systems, (b) new surveillance technology, and (c) all intelligence activities which might endanger individual's rights; rotating membership for Committee members; and limits on the length of time any staff member may work for the Committee. [Board Minutes, December 6-7, 1975, February 14-15, 1976, March 5-6, 1977.]

***

Further Information (not policy)

In *United States v. Richardson*, (1974), the Supreme Court denied standing to a taxpayer who claimed that the refusal of the executive branch to reveal the expenditures of the Central Intelligence Agency violated the statement and account clause of the Constitution.

Organizational Expression

Policy #119

Federal Lobbying Laws

In 1971 the Union supported legislation which would permit non-profit, tax-exempt organizations, to which contributions are tax-deductible under Section 501(c)(3) of the Internal Revenue Service laws, to communicate directly with Congress and state legislatures on matters related to these organizations' interests, without jeopardizing their tax-deductible status. IRS prohibitions on 501(c)(3) organizations do not apply to business organizations which can deduct "ordinary and necessary" expenses incurred in furthering their private economic gain, including expenditures for lobbying. Non-profit organizations under Section 501(c)(3), which include many civil rights, poverty, conservation, consumer and other "public interest" groups and law firms, should be placed on an equal footing with business associations and other 501(c) organizations in their ability to present their views and expertise to Congress and the state legislatures. This statement, while allowing groups that seek support from the general public to lobby without endangering their tax status (tax-deductibility for donor contributions) did not cover two important aspects of the issue; 1) whether other groups, such as private foundations, chambers of commerce, and civil leagues should be treated similarly with respect to their tax status; and 2) whether the existing prohibitions on Section 501(c)(3) organizations prevented "grassroots" or indirect lobbying, such as letter-writing campaigns. In 1976, the ACLU decided that all organizations should not lose the right to receive tax-deductible contributions because of lobbying activity, be it direct or indirect. Such lobbying is regarded as an exercise of First Amendment rights. [Board Minutes, October 2-3, 1971 and June 9, 1976.]

Policy #120

Regulation of Lobbyists

The ACLU opposes the requirement of disclosure, under the 1946 Federal Regulation of Lobbying Act, of names of persons who contribute $500 or more to organizations that lobby.

The public has a right to know the identity of persons and groups who substantially engage in lobbying and bring pressure on legislators to influence legislation. Legislators themselves are especially helped by such identifications because so much of the information and political appraisals they receive come from representatives of special interest groups purporting to advance the public interest.

The existing Federal Regulation of Lobbying Act of 1946, as narrowly construed by the Supreme Court in *United States v. Harriss* (1954), has been held to be constitutional. That Act, as now construed, covers only direct lobbying activities with members of Congress or its committees by persons who have solicited, collected or received contributions with the intended purpose to influence the passage or defeat of legislation by Congress.

Any proposed lobbying legislation must be responsive to First Amendment rights. It must not curb dissent, harass grassroots lobbying, or compel registration and membership disclosure by political organizations.

Since the time of the *Harriss* case, the Supreme Court has become properly sensitive to these concerns, and has struck down a number of registration requirements, notably at the instance of the NAACP complaining of state legislation that had repressive intentions.

Some proposals currently before Congress are so sweeping in their definitions of "lobbyists," and are so onerous in their requirements of recordkeeping and reporting, that such legislation would be a real threat to freedom of speech under the First Amendment.

Because of the important First Amendment interests which must be weighed against the public's right to know, regulation of lobbyists, in our judgment, should be confined to the following obligations of registration, reporting, and disclosure:

1) The identity of lobbyists, that is, the persons or organizations that collect or receive contributions for the purpose of influencing legislation by direct communication with members of the legislature.

2) The identity of substantial contributors to lobbying activities (with substantiality measured in thousands rather than hundreds of dollars).

3) The primary subjects and measures to which lobbying is directed.

4) The clients for whom the lobbying is carried on. This requirement may not be applied so as to require reporting or disclosure of good faith individual membership in organizations that lobby or support lobbying, other than substantial contributors, as in paragraph two above.

5) The annual aggregate of such lobbying expenditures. [Board Minutes, October 2-3, 1976.]

Nuclear Energy

Policy #121

Nuclear and Other Energy Programs

The ACLU opposes the licensing and operation of any facility designed to convert and deliver energy to consumers where governmental suppression of information or the infringement of any constitutional guarantee accompanies the licensing and/or operation of the facility or of associated facilities.[1] Before a license is granted for the operation of any energy facility, a comprehensive statement should be presented showing that protection of civil liberties has been considered and implemented. [Board Minutes, April 10-11, 1976.] (See also policies on Access to Government Information and Nuclear Tests.)

---

[1] The ACLU supports the following proposed due process safeguards in adjudicatory or rulemaking proceedings affecting energy programs: Right to a Hearing, Right to Notice, Right to Counsel, Right to Discovery, Right to a Written Record of the Proceedings, Right to a Written Decision, Right to a Decision based on the Record, and Right to an Impartial Decision Maker. A further description of these statements is available upon request from the national office.

DUE PROCESS OF LAW

Police Practices

Policy #208

Federal Aid for Law Enforcement Techniques

All attempts to make police operations more efficient and effective, within the scope of what is constitutionally permissible, should be encouraged and fostered. For this reason the ACLU favors legislation providing federal aid to state and local governments for police recruitment and training facilities and for projects and experiments in techniques of law enforcement, crime detection and prevention, and correction. It is vital to the preservation of our civil liberties not only to stem an increasing crime rate but also, and equally, to have police officers who are trained to know and respect the constitutional rights of all those with whom they deal. [Board Minutes, October 21, 1963; ACLU Statement before Senate Committee on the Judiciary, July 30, 1965.] POLICY UNDER REVIEW.

The ACLU urges that federal aid be used to divert state and local law enforcement agencies from their preoccupation with victimless crimes. (See policy on Data Collection, Storage, and Dissemination.) The ACLU objects to the use of federal funds to expand the data gathering practices of state and local law enforcement agencies which intrude on privacy. The ACLU criticizes the federal Law Enforcement Assistance Administration for failing to obey a legislative mandate to deny funds to state and local police departments which discriminate on grounds of race and sex in their employment policies. [ACLU Statement before U.S. Senate Subcommittee on Criminal Laws and Procedures, October 23, 1975.]

Policy #210

Prostitution

The ACLU supports the decriminalization of prostitution and opposes state regulation of prostitution. The ACLU also condemns the abuse of vagrancy or loitering laws of licensing or regulatory schemes to harass and arrest those who may be engaged in solicitation for prostitution. While there are both male and female prostitutes, laws against prostitution most frequently refer to, or are applied to, women. Despite the statutory stress on female prostitution, the ACLU's policy is applicable to prostitutes of both sexes. (See policy on Homosexuality.)

65

Such laws have traditionally represented one of the most direct forms of discrimination against women. The woman who engages in prostitution is punished criminally and stigmatized socially while her male customer, either by the explicit design of the statute or through a pattern of discriminatory enforcement, is left unscathed.

Prostitution laws are also a violation of the right of individual privacy because they impose penal sanctions for the private sexual conduct of consenting adults. Whether a person chooses to engage in sexual activity for purposes of recreation, or in exchange for something of value, is a matter of individual choice, not for governmental interference. Police use of entrapment techniques to enforce laws against this essentially private activity are reprehensible. Similarly, the use of loitering and vagrancy laws to punish prostitutes for their status or to make arrests on the basis of reputation and appearance, is contrary to civilized notions of due process of law. [Board Minutes, September 27-28, 1975.]

Since the ACLU policy is that prostitution should not be made criminal, solicitation for prostitution is entitled to the protection of the First Amendment. [Board Minutes, April 10-11, 1976.]

The ACLU reaffirms its policy favoring removal of criminal penalties for prostitution, and in support of total sexual freedom among consenting adults in private. [Board Minutes, March 5-6, 1977.]

Policy #215

Alcoholism and Public Drunkenness

The ACLU takes the position that public drunkenness is not itself a sufficient justification for the deprivation of personal liberty. Laws prohibiting public drunkenness seek to penalize mere offensiveness, and, therefore, exceed the proper limits of legal sanctions.

Involuntary civil commitment for alcoholism is a violation of individual rights. The individual should be allowed to refuse any treatment for drunkenness or alcoholism. In the case of public drunkenness, an individual should be allowed to refuse emergency treatment or "protective custody" including transportation to a treatment facility. There is no objection on civil liberties grounds to emergency treatment without consent of an individual who has become unconscious from alcohol.

This policy does not preclude the punishment of behavior by intoxicated persons which is also prohibited for sober persons, e.g. assaultive behavior. The criminal liability of intoxicated persons for such behavior should be determined according to the principles of criminal responsibility.

In some types of situations, narrowly drawn laws might have to single out acts of drunken persons; for example, activities that are unusually dangerous when performed by persons in drunken states (e.g., driving). [Board Minutes, March 5-6, 1977.]

Policy #229

Sexual Assault Laws

The American Civil Liberties Union believes that society's reaction to the crime of sexual assault has been pervaded with attitudes and assumptions which are contrary to our notion of fairness. This has elevated the crime to a near-mystical status and spawned a set of practices which, in the annals of criminal law, are unique to sexual assault.

As ACLU and its affiliates attempt to influence the passage of legislation which reflects civil liberties concerns, we will call attention to the following areas, in which the interests of due process and equal treatment under the law would be better served by the institution of reforms of the kind we suggest.

Definition

The word "rape" itself is charged with emotion, and does not serve to cover the many varieties of sexual crimes. ACLU prefers the use of the term "sexual assault," a sex-neutral definition which would afford equal protection to both men and women, and which include an entire range of forcible sex acts, which can then be distinguished in degree and kind (i.e., laws may distinguish degrees of force and coercion—threats with a deadly weapon, verbal threats, etc.). Sex neutral laws would also provide protection to the many men who are the victims of frequent sexual abuse in prisons and elsewhere.

Spousal Relationships

The existence of the married state should not be a bar to prosecution, but may be introduced in evidence. Laws which prohibit prosecution when the complainant is the spouse of the defendant should be eliminated.

Treatment of Victims

Sexual assault victims should be treated no differently from victims of other crimes. Sexual assault victims are often treated with skepticism and abuse at the hands of law enforcement and health services personnel. This treatment ranges from official disbelief and insensitivity to cruel and harsh probes of the victim's lifestyle and motivation. Such abrogation of responsibility by institutions meant to assist and protect victims of crime can only compound the trauma of the victim's original experience. ACLU supports affirmative programs to train personnel in police departments, prosecutors' offices and hospitals in more sensitive and effective response to sexual assault. Medical institutions should be especially careful to preserve records and data for possible use as evidence.

Sentencing

Penalties for crime reflect society's sense of outrage, and its view of sexual assault has been demonstrated in the sentencing provisions of the law. ACLU believes that society's interest in protecting its citizens from sexual assault would be better served by less severe penalties. To the extent that legally prescribed sexual assault penalties are disproportionate to the penalties prescribed for other aggravated assaults, they should be brought into line with penalties for other kinds of aggravated assaults. [Board Minutes, March 5-6, 1977.]

Use of Prior Sexual History in Rape Trials

There is in many rape cases a potential conflict between the right of the defendant to a fair trial and the complainant's right to have his or her claim to protection of the law vindicated without undue invasion of sexual privacy. In many cases this conflict may be irresolvable, and when that is the case the right to a fair trial should not be qualified, no matter how compelling the countervailing concerns. However, careful application by trial judges of the proper standards of relevance of testimony, control of cross-examination and argument, and elimination of prejudicial instructions unique to rape and similar cases could do much to preserve rape complainants from unnecessary imposition upon their rights to sexual privacy, without detracting from the fairness of the trial. Closed hearings should be used to ascertain the relevance of any proposed line of testimony or cross-examination that may involve a witness' prior sexual history. The determination of relevance or irrelevance should be stated by the court on the record along with its reasons for so holding.

A determination as to the relevance of the prior sexual history of either the complainant or the defendant in rape[1] cases are acceptable only if it is administered fairly and free from sexist assumptions. Subject to special evidentiary rules designed to protect defendants for reasons other than relevance, the criteria for admitting evidence of prior sexual history employed in rape cases must apply equally to the prosecution and the defense. Similarly, any pre-trial screening process must apply equally to the prosecution and the defense.

Some aspects of some current rape laws clearly do not meet minimum standards of acceptability. Even where the defense is consent, the prosecution should not be permitted, as a matter of course, to introduce evidence of the complainant's prior chastity; neither should the defense, without more, be

---

[1] While sexist assumptions and practices cause harm most often to victims of rape or attempted rape, their rights can be protected if rape is treated as but one form of sexual assault by statutes and courts. We therefore urge that standards and procedures be developed to apply to all forms of sexual assault and that the phrase "sexual assault" be used instead of "rape" in policy statements, laws, etc., in order to remove special legal disabilities from rape complainants.

permitted to prove the complainant's prior unchastity. "Unchaste witness" instructions which permit an inference of lessened credibility from the fact of prior sexual activity are based on no rational inference and violate a complainant's right to sexual privacy—just as a "chaste witness" instruction would violate a defendant's right to a fair trial if invoked by the prosecution. A statute, for example, which makes admissible evidence tending to prove that the complainant has been convicted of a prostitution offense, or even evidence concerning prior consensual sexual relations between the complainant and the defendant, without the necessity of showing a particular relevance, unconstitutionally infringes on the right to sexual privacy of such complainants. [Board Minutes, February 14-15, 1976.]

Policy #233

Discovery Costs in Government Secrecy Cases

The government should pay all costs, including fees, transcripts, depositions, and copying fees, arising out of discovery in any case where it is alleged that the government is withholding or keeping secret information which would, if disclosed, reveal illegal acts by government or government officials. This is particularly aimed at the costs of copying materials produced as the result of discovery in such cases. [Board Minutes, March 5-6, 1977.]

Policy #234

Capital Punishment

The ACLU opposes the death penalty because it denies equal protection of the laws, is cruel and unusual punishment, and removes guarantees of due process of law. The death penalty is so inconsistent with the underlying values of our democratic system—the pursuit of life, liberty, and happiness—that the imposition of the death penalty for any crime is a denial of civil liberties. The Union believes that past court decisions to the contrary are in error, and will seek the repeal of existing laws imposing the death penalty and reversal of convictions carrying a sentence of death.

The existence of the death penalty for crimes results in discrimination against the poor, the uneducated, and members of minority communities. Its imposition as the result of racial bias is easily demonstrated by the statistics on executions from 1930 to the present.[1] The greater likelihood of its imposition upon the poor is demonstrated by unimpeachable statistical analysis and arises among other things from the obvious fact that the financially able accused of a crime may employ legal counsel and compensate them fully for the extensive efforts necessary to pursue the many remedies available to those under penalty of death. But the poor, although they too have the right to counsel, have only that counsel which is volunteered, or which is compensated by the state. It is unrealistic to believe that such counsel, while dedicated, can give the kind, range, and detail of service given by counsel compensated at the usual rate paid our most competent lawyers.

Thus, in the case of the death penalty, the punishment does not fit the crime. It is, in fact, a constitutionally prohibited denial of equal protection of the law because it results—regardless of the written provisions of statutes permitting it—in imposition of the death penalty almost exclusively upon society's most disadvantaged members.

The Union also believes that contemporary ideas of the significance of human life make imposition of the death penalty cruel and unusual punishment, which is prohibited by the Constitution. To retain the theory that the death penalty is not cruel is to ignore the persistence of individual and collective conscience which says that death imposed by the force of the state is the ultimate cruelty upon the person whose life is taken. General public abhorrence of the death penalty is revealed by the prohibition or narrow limitation of capital punishment in *statutes*, and by the frequent reversal of guilty verdicts for technical errors which to laymen and lawyers both seem simply to reflect the courts' apprehension that to permit the judgment to stand would result in the ending of a life.

The irreversibility of the death penalty means that error discovered after the penalty has been imposed cannot be corrected. One who suffers the death penalty, and subsequently is found to have been improperly convicted, has been denied due process of law. Moreover, because jury panels in capital cases are selected partly on the basis of a belief in the death penalty, the state is protected against a jury biased against capital punishment, but the defendant is not protected against a jury biased in favor of it. So too does the existence of the death penalty have a deleterious effect on the administration of justice. The incentive of a capital conviction acts as a spur to the use of unfair or even lawless methods by police and prosecutors, to which is added blatant and emotional coverage by the mass media, all combining to make a fair trial impossible. [Board Minutes, October 2-3, 1976.]

---

[1] Of the 3,859 persons executed for all crimes since 1930, 54.6% have been black or members of other racial minority groups. Of the 455 executed for rape alone, 89.5% have been non-white. As census data clearly reveal, blacks in American society have consistently represented approximately 10% of the United States population. (Source: Bureau of Prisons, National Prisoner Statistics, Bulletin No. 45, *Capital Punishment 1930-68*, August 1969.) Of the 392 persons on death row on August 1, 1977, 50.8% were non-white, continuing the classic pattern of racially discriminatory imposition of the death penalty. (Source: Death-row Census, August 1, 1977, National Coalition Against the Death Penalty.)

Further Information (not policy)

In the 1972 decision in *Furman v. Georgia*, the Supreme Court had ruled that absolute discretion on the part of the sentencing authority (judge and/or jury) to impose the death penalty or life imprisonment for a capital crime was a violation of the Eighth Amendment bar against cruel and unusual punishment. The Court thereby struck down virtually all the then existing state death-penalty statutes. The Court, however, failed to rule on the underlying question of whether a capital punishment was inherently unconstitutional. Some 36 states thereupon enacted new statutes, providing either for the mandatory imposition of the death penalty for capital crimes or setting forth certain criteria to be considered by the sentencing authority before choosing between the death sentence or life imprisonment.

In 1976, the Supreme Court held that the death penalty did not invariably violate the Eighth Amendment. It held constitutional a number of state capital statutes that provide for a separate post-conviction sentencing hearing ("bifurcated trial") at which the jury chooses between a life imprisonment or death sentence after considering the aggravating and mitigating circumstances of the particular case ("guided discretion statutes"), *Gregg v. Georgia; Proffitt v. Florida;* and *Jurek v. Texas.* The availability of appeal of the death sentence was declared another requisite of a constitutionally valid death-penalty law. At the same time, the Supreme Court held that death-penalty laws that provide for the mandatory death penalty upon conviction for certain crimes were unconstitutional, *Woodson v. North Carolina; Roberts v. Louisiana.* Subsequent to these decisions, the Supreme Court held in *Coker v. Georgia* (1977), that the death penalty could not constitutionally be imposed for a non-homicidal rape of an adult female, nor mandatorily for the killing of a police officer in the performance of his duty, *Roberts v. Louisiana II* (1977). The Court is expected to rule shortly on whether capital punishment is constitutionally permissible for felony murder where the defendant did not directly commit the homicide.

The Supreme Court has now clearly ruled that capital punishment is permissible 1) for murder committed by the defendant, 2) where the sentencing involves a jury process of considering the aggravating and mitigating circumstances of the particular case and 3) where the death sentence is appealable. It is not known whether the Court would hold traditional capital but non-homicidal crimes (such as treason and espionage) to be constitutionally punishable by death.

Numerous states have amended their capital statutes to conform to the *Gregg* et al. holdings, and 34 states now have death-penalty laws on the books. Congress is in the process of rewriting the death-penalty provisions of the Federal Criminal Code to conform to the Supreme Court's guidelines. At March 1, 1978 over 440 persons were under sentence of death in 24 states, but only one person (Gary Mark Gilmore, Utah) had actually been executed since the *Gregg* decisions. The marked racial bias in the imposition of the death penalty continues unchanged, with about half the people on death row from minority communities. Current research tends to bear out that racial discrimination in capital punishment extends also to the race of the victim of the murder, the overwhelming majority of persons sentenced to death having killed white victims.

Policy #236

Prisoners, Parolees, and Ex-Convicts

(a) Prisoners remain subject to the Constitution and while incarcerated should suffer only restrictions of those constitutional rights which are necessary concomitants to the valid purpose of incarceration.

When the state incarcerates an individual, it takes responsibility for that person's fair, safe, and humane treatment as state action pursuant to the Fifth or Fourteenth Amendments, and it is forbidden cruel and unusual punishment by the Eighth Amendment. Yet the National Commission on the Causes and Prevention of Crime has cited "scandalous conditions" existing in the nation's jails and prisons. Such conditions violate the rights of prisoners to the decency and respect to which they are entitled even when they are being punished by the state.

But the state is obliged to offer more than humane punishment to a prisoner. Society expects that upon release from prisons an individual will be able to function as a law-abiding and productive citizen; and it looks to the state to rehabilitate prisoners in preparation for this role. Nevertheless, according to the Commission, jails and prisons "have been indicted as crime breeding institutions." The public's growing concern with the apparently rising incidence of crime, much of which is recidivism, is an indication of a need to find truly effective methods of rehabilitation. Yet the Commission found that "programs of rehabilitation are shallow and dominated by greater concern for punishment and custody than for corrections. Thus correctional administrators are often said to be presiding over schools in crime." It is time to reverse the emphasis of correctional institutions from "greater concern for punishment and custody" to greater concern for rehabilitation. Such an effort is essential to reduce crime and the violence it spawns. For crime and violence too easily become the basis for official actions which directly violate basic civil liberties.

Indeed, punishment ought not to be a part of the purpose of pretrial detention that results when an accused is unable to make bail. (See policy on Bail.) In the small number of cases where pretrial release is not possible, every effort should be made to remove the punitive aspects of pre-trial detention in keeping with the presumption of innocence.

The opportunity for rehabilitation is undermined and the civil liberties of ex-convicts violated by broad and unjustified disabilities imposed upon ex-convicts and unrelated to any legitimate state interest. Society must absorb ex-convicts and offer them the chance for productive work and dignity or expect that they will return to crime. Thus, blanket denials of the opportunity for government employment or the right to vote, for example, impose additional punishment on the ex-convict and run against society's interest in increasing the person's alternatives to criminal activities. [Board Minutes, December 5-7, 1969, September 24-25, 1977.]

***

(b) Among the specific rights to which the Union believes that prisoners are constitutionally entitled are protection from physical mistreatment by guards or by other inmates and the guarantee of essential medical care. In addition to a ban on censorship of a prisoner's literary writings, there should be a prohibition of censorship of the personal content of a prisoner's letters or other written communications with an attorney. Nor should listening devices be permitted in visiting booths. (See also policy on Electronic Eavesdropping regarding the use of TV surveillance in jails.)

The courts have already established that prisoners have a right to their own religious beliefs. Although it recognizes the necessity for administrative judgment in this area, ACLU is concerned about prison practices which, in effect, discriminate between religions, punish inmates because of their beliefs, and unduly restrict access to religious facilities, services, and documents. (See policy on Prison Chaplaincy.)

In order to implement the acknowledged right to due process, the prisoner must have access either to outside counsel or to prison writ writers (if the prisoner is personally unable to function in that capacity, and must not be punished for seeking such assistance. The courts have already acknowledged that the prisoner has an unabridged right to apply to a federal court for a writ of habeas corpus, but in practice this right has been impaired by numerous obstructive acts of prison administrators and is ultimately frustrated by the denial of effective counsel. [Board Minutes, December 5-7, 1969.]

***

(c) A parolee is entitled to these procedural rights before his or her parole can be revoked: the provision of legal counsel where he or she is unable to pay, opportunity to confront and cross-examine witnesses, and the right to examine adverse documentary evidence. These procedures are all traditionally associated with the concepts of due process of law and the right to a full and fair hearing as prerequisites to the imposition of punishment. [News Release, September 23, 1963.]

A parole board must not make any distinction between political and other types of offenders. [Board Minutes, August 27, 1951.]

***

(d) The Union opposes municipal crime registration ordinances because they impose additional penalties for crimes for which individuals have already been penalized by the criminal law. They also discriminate against ex-convicts who have already served their sentences and could easily be used to harass such persons, thus preventing their rehabilitation. Moreover, the effectiveness of registration as a crime prevention measure is open to serious doubt, based on the experience of European countries where the identification card system has operated for years and has apparently done little to reduce crime. [Board Minutes, May 21, 1951; Weekly Bulletin, January 18, 1965.] (See also part a, above, and policy on Non-Resident Employee Registration.)

POLICY UNDER REVIEW.

***

Further Information (not policy)

Since 1969 the Supreme Court has handed down a number of significant decisions affecting prisoners' rights. In *Haines v. Kerner* (1972) a prisoner brought a damages action against officials who allegedly acted in an unconstitutional manner in placing the plaintiff in solitary confinement as a disciplinary measure. The Court concluded that in this situation the plaintiff could not be deprived of his liberty without due process. The Court also stated that the *pro se* complaints of a prisoner should be held to a less demanding standard than those drafted by attorneys.

In *Morrissey v. Brewer* (1972) the Court said that the revocation of parole inflicts a loss of liberty entitling the parolee to procedural due process protections prior to revocation. The parolee was required to receive a preliminary hearing. If probable cause was shown at that hearing the parolee was entitled to a final revocation hearing at which he or she would receive a number of due process protections, including written notice of the alleged violations, disclosure of the evidence against the parolee, an opportunity to be heard and the qualified right to confront and cross-examine the witnesses against the parolee. In *Gagnon v. Scarpelli* (1973) the Court held that revocation of probation also results in a loss of a liberty to which due process protections attach. The Court also decided that the right to counsel in parole and probation revocations would be determined on a case by case basis. *Wolff v. McDonnell* (1974) extended due process protections to the deprivation of "good time." Although the due process requirements mandated here were less stringent than those of *Morrissey*, they still included the right to call witnesses and to present documentary evidence, where such evidence is not hazardous to institutional safety or correctional goals.

In *McGinnis v. Roysten* (1973), the Court rejected an equal protection challenge to a statute which calculated good time credit and parole eligibility from the date of sentencing. Plaintiffs argued that this discriminated between persons who were incarcerated before sentence in a county jail and those who were not. The Court said that good time is awarded after the prisoner's rehabilitation has been evaluated by the Corrections Department. Where there are no corrective or rehabilitative services in the county jail, there can be no evaluation upon which to base a good time calculation. Hence no equal protection violation was found.

Wilwording v. Swenson (1971) involved the issue of exhaustion of remedies in habeas corpus cases. Here prisoners challenged their living conditions and disciplinary measures while in maximum security, but did not seek their release. The Court ruled that when state habeas corpus procedures had been exhausted, the plaintiff was not required to attempt to use alternative state remedies.

In *Johnson v. Avery* (1973) the Court held that until the state provided a reasonable alternative to assist prisoners in preparing post-conviction petitions, it could not bar prisoners from assisting other prisoners in preparing *habeas* petitions. To do so would deny poorly educated prisoners access to the courts.

In *Wolff v. McDonnell*, (see above) the Court said that the state could require that mail be marked as originating from an attorney, but that the mail could only be opened in the prisoner's presence and could not be read by prison officials. In *Procunier v. Martinez* (1974) the Court delineated these criteria in determining whether censorship of prisoner mail violated the First Amendment. "(1) The regulation or practice in question must further an important or substantial government interest unrelated to the suppression of expression . . . (2) The limitation of First Amendment freedoms must be narrowly drawn and no greater than necessary to protect the government interest involved. (3) The regulations must be applied objectively and not invite prison officials to apply their own personal prejudices." In *Procunier v. Navarette* (1977), the Court held that state prison officials have a qualified immunity from damage actions for the negligent mishandling of a prisoner's outgoing mail.

Pell v. Procunier (1974) and *Saxbe v. Washington Post Co.* (1974) deal with a state and federal regulation which banned interviews with specific incarcerated individuals. Exceptions to the regulations allowed family members, friends, clergy and attorneys to see these individuals. The Court ruled that since alternative communication channels were open to the prisoners (i.e. family, mail) their First Amendment rights were not violated. In *Saxbe*, the Court declared that the press was not denied access to information available to the general public, and that information on prison conditions was available from alternative sources. Hence the First Amendment rights of the press were not violated.

In *Cruz v. Beto* (1972) the Court held that a practice denying a Buddist prisoner a reasonable opportunity to practice his religion, while such an opportunity was given to members of major religions, violated the First and Fourteenth Amendments.

Two companion cases clarify due process issues that were unresolved in *Wolff v. McDonnell.* In *Baxter v. Palmigiano* (1976), the Court held that a prisoner does not have the right to cross-examine witnesses or to have retained or appointed counsel at a disciplinary hearing, even though he might also be subject to new criminal charges. The second case, *Enomoto v. Clutchette*, held that the *Wolff* procedures are not available to a prisoner who has lost privileges of relatively less importance than solitary confinement or loss of good time. In *Meachum v. Fano* (1976), the Court held that prisoners have no procedural due process rights prior to their reclassification or transfer to a higher security prison. However, in a subsequent case, the Court suggested that a transfer designed to penalize the prisoner for engaging in otherwise protected First Amendment activity might not be valid, *Montanye v. Haymes*, (1976). In the area of medical treatment, the Court held that deliberate indifference to the injuries of prisoners violates the Eighth Amendment's proscription against cruel and unusual punishment, *Estelle v. Gamble*, (1976).

Bounds v. Smith (1977), held that the constitutional right of access to the courts requires that state prison authorities provide inmates with adequate law libraries or assistance from persons trained in the law.

The efforts to organize prisoners into unions was dealt a severe blow by *Jones v. North Carolina Prisoners' Union, Inc.* (1977). The Supreme Court held that state regulations prohibiting union meetings and the solicitation of union membership did not violate the First Amendment or the equal protection clause.

Policy #237

Criminal Sentences

Deprivation of an individual's physical freedom is one of the most severe interferences with liberty that the state can impose. Moreover, imprisonment is harsh, frequently counter-productive, and costly. There is, therefore, a heavy burden of justification on the imposition of a prison sentence.

A suspended sentence with probation should be the preferred form of treatment, to be chosen always unless the circumstances plainly call for greater severity. Moreover, if some form of present punishment is called for, a fine should always be the preferred form of the penalty, unless the circumstances plainly call for a prison sentence.

The most appropriate correctional approach is re-integrating the offender into the community, and the goals of re-integration are furthered much more readily by working with an offender in the community than by incarceration.

Probation should be authorized by the legislature in every case, exceptions to the principle are not favored, and any exceptions if made, should be limited to the most serious offenses, such as murder or treason.

Probation is preferable to imprisonment for five reasons:

First, probation maximizes the liberty of the individual, while at the same time vindicating the authority of the law and effectively protecting the public from further violations of law. Second, assuming that rehabilitation is a feasible goal, probation affirmatively promotes the rehabilitation of the offender by continuing normal community contacts. Third, probation avoids the negative and frequently stultifying effects of confinement which often severely and unnecessarily complicate the re-integration of the offender into the community. Fourth, probation greatly reduces the financial costs to the public treasury. Fifth, probation minimizes the impact of the conviction upon innocent dependents of the offender.

For those weighty reasons, the harsh, counter-productive, and costly sentence of imprisonment is strongly disfavored and carries a heavy burden of justification by the government.

The ACLU opposes indeterminate sentences, and sentences which violate principles of proportionality.

The ACLU also opposes confining people in prison or determining the duration of confinement for the purpose of rehabilitating them (that is, making them better persons). We favor the provision of opportunities for self-improvement to persons confined in prison on other grounds.

Because the efficacy of general deterrence has not been established, and because it involves punishment of one person for the benefit of others, the ACLU opposes general deterrence as the basis for incarceration.

The ACLU believes that what will deter future criminal behavior by the criminal (specific deterrence) and criminal behavior by others (general deterrence) is not known. It is quite uncertain that prohibited conduct is more effectively deterred as punishment is made more severe. The goal of deterrence, therefore, is not a justification for a harsh sentencing structure. Indeed, because excessive penalties are often mitigated in practice by sporadic enforcement, their effect is to detract from purported deterrence.

The sentence should be determined at the conclusion of the trial. To minimize disparate sentences for comparable crimes in comparable circumstances, sentencing discretion should be restricted by legislative or judicially determined guidelines describing aggravating and mitigating circumstances. Since the ACLU views incarceration as the penalty of last resort to be imposed only when no less restrictive alternative is appropriate, the ACLU opposes mandatory sentencing schemes that do not allow for non-incarcerative options. In any case where incarceration is a possible penalty, the reasons for the sentence shall be stated in open court and on the record. Sentences shall be subject to appellate review at the behest of the defendant. [Board Minutes, March 4-5, 1978.] (See policy on Prisoners, Parolees, and Ex-Convicts.)

The Mentally Ill

Policy #238

Civil Commitment

Introductory Statement

Mental illness can never *by itself* be a justifiable reason for depriving a person of liberty against his or her objection. [Board Minutes, December 5-7, 1969, ACLU Statement before Senate Subcommittee on Constitutional Rights, May 8, 1963.]

This *limited* position did not deal with specific standards for commitment and was not overruled when the Board rejected a position arguing that persons could never be commited on any ground. In 1977, the Board instead said that the ACLU takes no further position on civil commitment. [Board Minutes, March 5-6, 1977.]

(a) Procedures Concerning Commitment of Persons to Mental Institutions

1) The individual has a right to counsel at every step of the proceeding, including subsequent periodic reviews. If the individual cannot select an attorney, counsel should be provided by the state. The attorney should be present at interviews between the individual and the physician which are relevant to the commitment proceedings. Selection of court-appointed counsel should be made in such a manner as to ensure the attorney's independence and effectiveness in representing the individual.

2) The individual should not be incarcerated prior to a hearing, except in an emergency for court-ordered psychiatric examination and observation for a period no longer than seventy-two hours.

In many states, individuals are committed under so-called emergency proceedings (the definition of what constitutes an emergency is in some cases very broad) without benefit of a hearing. In such cases a hearing should be held within a seventy-two hour period. The hearing must be mandatory and not dependent on the individual's request for it. Failure to request a hearing cannot be deemed a waiver. During such periods of emergency commitment, no action should be taken on the person which might have a permanent effect, and the use of drugs should be limited solely to those deemed by the attending physician to be medically essential to reasonable custody prior to the hearing, and further, should be so limited as not to interfere with the patient's ability to recognize his or her status and effectively contest or otherwise deal with the subject, including participation in a hearing. The patient should not be or appear to be drugged or tranquilized at a hearing.

Persons being held pending judicial commitment proceedings have not been adjudicated mentally ill. Due process of law requires that such persons must have full opportunity to prepare for the commitment proceedings and make an informed defense. Accordingly, hospitals, institutions, or holding facilities have an affirmative obligation to provide unrestricted mail, telephone communications, personal visits with attorneys, medical personnel and others of the proposed patient's choice.

3) While the hearing in a civil commitment proceeding need not necessarily take on the physical appearance of a trial, the fundamental rights guaranteed under due process must be preserved. The hearing should be held in an open courtroom, whether in or outside of a hospital. The individual must have a jury hearing unless he chooses to waive the right. The jury should be instructed that it is not simply to accept as truth whatever the psychiatrists have determined. The judge should carefully instruct the jury on the relevant criteria for commitment, insuring the use of defined standards and compelling medical professionals to be specific when verbalizing their reasons for recommending commitment.

4) The individual shall be present at the hearing. If the hearing should take place after commitment, the individual should not be or appear to be heavily drugged or tranquilized. If drugs have been administered, the jury, on request of the patient's counsel, must be informed of the fact and of the probable effect of the drugs. If the hearing is held in a hospital, the individual should not appear in hospital attire, as this might prejudice the jury against his or her case.

5) The individual should receive written notice of the hearing and should have access to all records relevant to his or her case. All persons providing information for commitment proceedings must be informed that the information will become part of the record and may be available to the patient.

6) The state must prove beyond a reasonable doubt the need for commitment and the absence of less drastic alternatives with an equal chance of correcting the individual's alleged malady. A less drastic alternative cannot be deemed unavailable because the individual lacks funds for treatment. The state is obligated to finance treatment in non-coercive settings before it invokes involuntary commitment proceedings.

7) A privilege analogous to the privilege against self-incrimination in criminal trials should be applied in commitment proceedings. Every court-appointed examiner must submit a separate written report for his or her examination, a copy of which must be made available to the individual and/or his or her counsel as soon as possible after the examination and, in any event, prior to the hearing.

8) All communications between an individual and his or her psychotherapist (whether or not the therapist is a physician) should be privileged, including communications relevant to an issue in a commitment proceeding.

9) The above privilege would not extend to persons other than a psychotherapist. In such an interview, however, the individual should be warned of the right to remain silent and that anything he or she says may be used against him or her in a commitment proceeding.

10) There should be mandatory reviews at the end of 30, 60 and 90 days and at periodic intervals (at least three but no more than six months) thereafter. In addition, the individual retains the right to initiate reviews of his or her hospitalization.

11) The individual should be allowed to refuse *any* treatment for mental illness, except such treatment as may be required to prevent the patient from being a danger to others; provided that the individual should be able to refuse psychosurgery on *any grounds* whatsoever.

12) The individual should have complete freedom in communicating with his or her attorney and with medical personnel. Access to mail should be unrestricted. Access to the telephone should be unrestricted, subject only to reasonable regulations uniformly applied, based on time of calling and frequency of calling.

13) Commitment should not be equated with incompetency.

No person should be deprived of his or her civil rights, such as the power to control assets, make contracts, vote, engage in occupations, and control other non-medical personal affairs, solely by reason of commitment. Deprivation of such rights can be brought about only as a result of a specific judicial hearing relative to the person's ability to exercise such rights, and the consequences thereof. Any deprivation should be terminated as soon as possible, and automatic review of the continued need for such deprivation must occur at frequent intervals. Review must also be available at the person's option.

14) The individual patient should not be coerced into performing labor. He or she should receive reasonable pay for work done.

15) Voluntary mental health hospitalization and/or treatment are clearly preferable and superior from a civil libertarian viewpoint. Voluntary care is to be encouraged and no person should be involuntarily committed without having been given a full and free opportunity to become a voluntary patient.

However, it must be noted that voluntary commitment is often effectuated through the use of coercive methods. Sometimes individuals are induced to become "voluntary" patients after being threatened with emergency commitment proceedings. In other instances, persons who have voluntarily entered a hospital will be involuntarily transferred to another, less desirable institution under a temporary commitment authorization.

Procedural safeguards, such as described above, should be established in order to ensure that coercion is not, in fact, applied in ostensibly voluntary processes. A person who has been voluntarily committed has the right to leave the hospital upon request.

All of the minimal rights enumerated above should be applicable to voluntarily committed persons.

***

(b) *Employment*

The right of privacy protects individuals seeking employment or licenses from being asked or having to answer questions relating to previous mental commitment, unless the specific position or license being sought can be demonstratively shown by the prospective employer or licensing agency directly to involve the public health or safety. In such cases, individuals have the right to submit proof attesting to their mental stability or to the inapplicability of their condition to the position being sought. In the event employment or licensing is denied or terminated, the employer must demonstratively prove that the prior history of the applicant constitutes a danger to the public health and/or safety. The ACLU urges that appropriate legislation be framed to guarantee procedural safeguards for the individual so affected.

***

(c) *Disclosure of Records*

Nothing in an individual's hospital record should be disclosed to anyone without his or her express informed, written consent or a court order. Before a court orders disclosure, the individual should have the opportunity to contest such an order with the assistance of counsel. Disclosure should not be ordered unless the court finds by clear and convincing evidence that the failure to disclose poses dangers to the physical safety of other persons. (See also policy on Medical Records.) [Board Minutes, June 16-17, 1973, December 8-9, 1973, April 20-21, 1974.]

***

Further Information (not policy)

In *O'Connor v. Donaldson* (1975) the Supreme Court held in an unanimous decision that "a finding of 'mental illness' alone cannot justify a state's locking a person up against his will and keeping him indefinitely in simple custodial confinement." The decision has been interpreted to mean that in the absence of a finding of dangerousness, a person cannot be held indefinitely without treatment. The Court did not decide whether a state may confine a non-dangerous individual for the purpose of providing treatment, as opposed to rendering mere custodial care.

Several major issues in this area remain undecided, including whether mentally ill persons who are dangerous to themselves or others have a right to treatment after being compulsorily confined, and whether a non-dangerous mentally ill person may be confined for treatment purposes.

Policy #261

Medical Experimentation on Human Beings

(a) Informed consent must be a prerequisite to medical experimentation, and must be voluntarily given.

***

(b) Informed consent minimally requires that the consenting party receive a written statement in lay language (to be filed with the research agency) describing:

1) the overall purpose of the experiment

2) what will be done to the research subject—procedures, administrations, treatments, etc.

3) what will not be done to the subject—e.g. withholding of treatment, etc.

4) the nature of the experimental substance(s) and procedures

5) the possible benefits, if any, to the subject

6) the possible harm or risk, if any, to the subject

7) other treatments available to the subject in lieu of the experiment

8) whatever other sequelae that are likely to arise from the experiment. [Board Minutes, February 9-10, 1974.]
POLICY UNDER REVIEW.

Policy #262

Intrusive Medical Questions on Job Applications

The legitimate interest of an employer or licensing authority in an employee's health extends only to the employee's ability satisfactorily to perform the job sought. This interest must be satisfied by the least intrusive means available. Irrespective of whether the examining physician is provided by the employer, the licensing authority, or the applicant, medical information gathered during the course of the examination shall be privileged and confidential, and shall not be revealed to the employer or licensing authority, which shall be entitled only to the physician's certification of the applicant's ability or inability properly to perform the job as described to the applicant and the examining physician. [Board Minutes, September 24-25, 1977.]

Policy #265

Euthanasia

Consensual euthanasia involves an act or an omission by a second person at the request of an individual for the termination of the latter's life when he or she is either terminally ill or totally and permanently disabled. The ACLU recognizes this form of euthanasia as a legitimate extension of the right of control over one's own body.

The ACLU urges that state legislatures make "living wills"[1] a legally effective means of indicating consent to euthanasia.

---

[1] A "living will" is a testimentary document prepared by an individual at any time in advance of a condition which renders the person incapable of requesting no treatment, the cessation of current treatment, or the actual taking of that person's life (euthanasia). The will states the intent of that person as to the treatment or lack of treatment to be provided in the event of such a condition. The question of changed intent of the person suggests that the person periodically update the "will." No state presently recognizes such a "will" as legally binding.

While the ACLU maintains that assistance in the act of consensual euthanasia is not illegal, it also maintains that such assistance, most often required of physicians, is not compulsory. Once such a request is made, given the circumstances indicated above the physician must either comply with the request or withdraw from the case and inform the individual of his or her right to request the services of another physician. Also, without regard to individual capacity for commiting suicide, physicians must respect the right of the terminally ill or the totally and permanently disabled to request the termination of all treatment[1] by complying with the request. [Board Minutes, December 4-5, 1976.]

Policy #268

Constitutional Conventions

The ACLU notes the movement within state governments to call a constitutional convention for the purpose of proposing a federal constitutional amendment to require sharing of federal revenues with the states. While the ACLU has no policy interest regarding revenue sharing, the Union is concerned with the possibility that a convention could adopt other measures weakening the guarantees of the Bill of Rights. Existing constitutional rules for constitutional conventions are sketchy, and the danger of a "run-away" convention does exist. The ACLU notes existing safeguards against this possibility: judicial review and the fact that Congress does not have to submit the convention's product for ratification if the product is not considered to be concerned with the call for the convention. The ACLU believes it should not simply oppose a convention on the fear that it might exceed its basic call since the people's right to hold such a convention, if there is widespread dissatisfaction with state or federal government, is basic.

The ACLU opposes the calling of any constitutional convention designed to abridge or narrow existing civil liberties as they are understood by the ACLU.

Any proposed congressional legislation concerning constitutional conventions must be subject to the most rigorous scrutiny in order to ensure that the convention is fairly structured, confines its deliberations to the subject of the call, and does not otherwise infringe upon established civil liberties. Congress should act to confirm the justiciability of questions arising under the amendatory process by state law. [Board Minutes, February 6-7, 1971 and October 2-3, 1971.]

(See policy on Equal Rights Amendment.)

---

[1] The right of persons to request the termination of treatment applies to all patients, not only those requesting euthanasia. The last sentence of the third paragraph is not seen as contradicting the stipulations for euthanasia in the first paragraph. The stipulations of the first paragraph pertain to the *omission* of treatment while the language of the third paragraph is addressed to the *withdrawal* of current treatment.

EQUALITY BEFORE THE LAW

Racial And Other Discrimination

Policy #301

Housing

(a) Discrimination in the rental, sale, or mortgaging of housing, public or private, based on race, color, sex, religion, national origin, political affiliation, alienage or illigitimacy, is a denial of basic civil rights. The ACLU believes that such discrimination should be challenged on constitutional grounds, when possible, and that it should in any case be prohibited by legislation.

Individuals shall be exempt from this provision only in relation to their intimately shared private living arrangements. Such living arrangements shall consist of the household of which the individual is actually a member, and shall not extend, for example, to two-family dwellings where separate living units are maintained. This exception is intended to provide for the minimum essential requirements of the rights of privacy and free association, without infringing unnecessarily upon the important right of all individuals to gain access to housing without being hampered by the application of improper discrimination criteria.

When the state, or any of its agencies or officials, is involved in the rental, sale or mortgaging of housing, whether that involvement is direct or indirect, its actions should be designed to impede racial segregation and to foster integration of all peoples. [Board Minutes, September 27-28, 1975.]

With respect to removing such discrimination from private housing, the degree of public interest at stake requires—in addition to education—that state or local governments should legally prohibit such discrimination in the sale or rental of private housing. But groups established in good faith for non-housing purposes—e.g., religious bodies or fraternal orders—should be permitted in good faith to limit to their members the sale or rental of housing accommodations provided specifically for their members. (However, neither the Union's National Office nor any affiliate, need oppose or refrain from supporting legislation prohibiting discrimination in private housing merely because it contains other exceptions. If such a question arises the Board of Directors should be asked for guidance.) [Board Minutes, May 11, 1959.]

POLICY UNDER REVIEW.

***

(b) The ACLU endorses legislation which would make it unlawful for a lending institution to refuse mortgage or home improvement loans on all or substantially all property in a particular geographical area solely or partly because of the racial or ethnic composition of the area. [Board Minutes, December 3-4, 1977.]

***

(c) The ACLU supports anti-blockbusting statutes which prohibit false or deceptive statements concerning changes in the racial, religious, or national origin character of a neighborhood, and/or the effect of those changes, made with the intent for commercial gain, to promote the sale of property. Also, the ACLU supports, in such cases, civil action by a damaged party or the suspension or cancellation of a broker's license. [Board Minutes, June 7, 1972.]

***

(d) Zoning and other land use controls may not be applied in a fashion which substantially conflict with the opportunity of low and moderate income persons to secure minimally adequate housing in an economically and racially integrated environment.

Exclusionary zoning and land use practices by government have become a major source of segregation, both racial and economic, in residential areas of the United States. The pattern of legally enforced segregation which has come to characterize our use of land conflicts radically with the goal of equal opportunity in employment as increasing numbers of business enterprises move to areas where there is no low and moderate income housing; so too, it conflicts with equal opportunity in education where whole cities are fast becoming either all black or white; so too, it conflicts with the goal of decent and integrated housing for all Americans, when segments of our population are confined to the crowded and sub-standard housing of our ghettos.

Local governments are creatures and delegates of the states. The state is constitutionally obliged to assure its citizens equal treatment—at the hands of the state and of its delegates. The delegation of local autonomy over matters of zoning and land use must be accompanied by legal assurances that the authority so delegated will not be employed so as to defeat the needs of whole classes of the state's citizens.

The ACLU believes that the state and its delegated agents may not establish a regime of restraints or policies which prevents the allocation of residential land to low and moderate income housing or which in any way discriminates against low or moderate income people. Utilizing federal, state, and local governmental powers such as land-use permits, grants, tax incentives, and traffic planning, government has the responsibility of positive action to encourage the development of racially and economically integrated communities. [Board Minutes, December 9-10, 1972.]

***

(e) Enforcement by state or local court injunction of racial restrictive covenants (agreements entered into by private individuals with regard to disposal of private housing to Negro owners or occupants) constitute state action prohibited by the due process and equal protection clauses of the Fourteenth

Amendment. Inasmuch as these covenants amount to racial zoning ordinances, state enforcement is prohibited regardless of the fact that the covenants do not originate through official action. The right of the individual property owner to dispose of personal property as individual interest or taste may dictate, and to enforce such right through governmental aid, is not involved in this case, and would not under ordinary circumstances raise any question of constitutionality. [ACLU amicus brief, *Shelley vs. Kraemer.* 1947.]

***

Policy #306

Employment

(a) In a free society, every individual should enjoy equal access to employment opportunities and to the means of self-advancement, without invidious discrimination. Invidious discrimination includes, of course, not only discrimination on the grounds of race, sex, religion, national origin, political persuasion or alienage: it is practiced whenever any person is denied the chance to hold a job or to receive education or training on the basis of some personal characteristic unrelated to job fitness or educational promise. All forms of invidious discrimination offend basic civil liberties, and the ACLU will take action against each of them in appropriate cases. For the present, the pervasive long-continued, intractable quality of employment and educational discrimination against racial minorities and women warrants the highest priority in the allocation of the ACLU's resources devoted to combatting discrimination.

The root concept of the principle of non-discrimination is that individuals should be treated individually, in accordance with their personal merits, achievements and potential, and not on the basis of the supposed attributes of any class or caste with which they may be identified. However, when discrimination—and particularly when discrimination in employment and education—has been long and widely practiced against a particular class, it cannot be satisfactorily eliminated merely by the prospective adoption of neutral, "color-blind" standards for selection among the applicants for available jobs or educational programs. Affirmative action is required to overcome the handicaps imposed by past discrimination of this sort; and, at the present time, affirmative action is especially demanded to increase the employment and the educational opportunities of racial minorities and women.

The precise form of an effective affirmative action program must depend upon the nature of the employment or educational role in question, the skills or aptitudes required for performance in that role, its susceptibility to in-service training that can develop the required skills, the numbers and characteristics of persons whose interests would be advanced by entry into the role, the extent of present under-representation of minorities and women in the role, its place in the over-all economy, and other factors. But as a general matter, affirmative action should include:

1) Special efforts to seek out and recruit qualified members of under-represented groups;

2) Review of all standards and qualifications used to screen applicants, and the abandonment of any standard or qualification that is not a reliable predictor of requisite performance;

3) Development of special measures for the prediction of requisite performance in the case of under-represented groups whose ability to demonstrate potential performance by conventional measures is impaired;

4) Involvement of members of under-represented groups in responsible administrative and policy-making positions in the applicant-selection process;

5) To the extent feasible, provision of a program of in-service training or compensatory education that is fully adequate to develop or upgrade the potential performance of under-represented groups in order to assure their retention and make the affirmative action program work in practice;

6) Financial assistance to members of under-represented groups to the extent necessary and feasible to permit them to take advantage of in-service training and compensatory education or to overcome other entry or retention problems; and

7) The use of "target" ratios and timetables as goals for periodic assessment of the success of the affirmative action program, together with clear lines of responsibility to assure that, if goals are not being met, efforts will be intensified.

Preference may also be given to members of under-represented groups on grounds of unique fitness for the employment or educational role in question. This sort of preference is justifiable under the general principle that distinctions made along the lines of job-related characteristics are not invidious. Claims that such characteristics as race and sex are job-related require close scrutiny under any circumstances. But the ACLU recognizes that they are advanced to support the preferential admission of long and substantially under-represented groups.

The ACLU is generally opposed to hiring or entrance quotas that fix numbers or percentages of particular classes or groups, and it will oppose any claim by those establishing such quotas that they are not subject to constitutional and legal limitations.

However, in specific situations in which discriminatory employment practices have not been eradicated by other measures, and in order to eradicate the effects of past discrimination and to increase the representation of substantially under-represented groups, the ACLU will support a requirement that a certain number of persons within a group which has suffered discrimination be employed within a particular timetable.

Particular methods of enforcement of the policies set forth above may give rise to problems beyond the scope of the policies themselves. For example, government enforcement of affirmative action requirements in academic employment may raise issues of academic freedom. Until further experience has refined these issues, the ACLU can only resolve them as appears appropriate in concrete situations.

The ACLU recognizes that the process by which people are distributed among jobs and educational opportunities in American society is subject to many influences besides discrimination. By the same token, the goal of the affirmative action program proposed above is not necessarily a perfectly balanced representation of minorities and women in each employment and educational situation. [Board Minutes, April 14-15, 1973; Press Release, April 18, 1973.]

***

(b) Individually identifiable victims of hiring discrimination should be granted retroactive or constructive seniority. Discrimination in employment cannot effectively be ended without dealing with the problem of inequitable effects of layoffs. ACLU supports the use of effective possible mechanisms to prevent the undoing of affirmative action policies through layoffs which fall most heavily on women and minorities.

The Fourteenth Amendment requires the ACLU to fight against the erosion of affirmative action gains. The ACLU asserts that affirmative action principles must apply equally to layoffs.[1] [Board Minutes, December 3-4, 1977.] (See also policies on Poverty and Employment and Education under Sex Discrimination.)

***

(c) The ACLU has long believed that no citizen should suffer discrimination in employment because of race, religion, or national origin. For this reason it has been for many years a proponent of a federal fair employment practices statute, applicable to employers and trade unions alike, so that the protection of federal law would be extended to the right of employment on the basis of ability regardless of race, religion, national origin, or ancestry.

The Union therefore supported the enactment of the equal employment opportunity section of the 1964 Civil Rights Act, which does not compel an employer to hire any particular person but bans only the practice of racial or religious discrimination in employment. However, the measure will be more effective if responsibility for enforcement is removed from the present commission and placed into the hands of a single administrator, whose formal complaints would be heard by an independent board equipped with power to issue cease-and-desist orders. [Minutes of Equality Committee, March 28, 1863; ACLU Statement on Civil Rights Legislation, July 24, 1963.]

---

[1] These two sentences were part of the seven resolutions on economic matters passed by the 1976 Biennial Conference. By provision of the ACLU Constitution, the Board must accept or reject a Biennial Conference resolution within eighteen months of the Conference adjournment. At the December 1977 Board meeting, these two resolutions were tabled, and in effect, this action makes the Biennial Conference resolutions ACLU policy.

The Union has also argued that a state fair employment law can be invoked to bar discrimination by an employer engaged in interstate commerce; in other words, that an employer cannot violate the fair employment policies of the state where the business is based merely because the business involves interstate commerce. [News Release, January 28, 1963.]

A state law governing the licensing of certain occupations that is so drawn—or so enforced—as to exclude from the privilege of a license any class of individual on account of race denies that individual access to a lawful occupation in violation of the equal protection clause of the Fourteenth Amendment and in contravention of the United Nations Charter. [ACLU amicus brief, *Takahishi vs. Fish and Game Commission*, 1947.]

(See also policy on Racial Discrimination and Fair Representation by Unions and Employment and Education.)

Policy #313

American Indians

General Policy

American Indian people and their tribes occupy a unique position in American society. Throughout the history of this country, Indian people have maintained cultural and religious identities distinct from those of all other peoples. American Indian tribes have continuously existed as self-governing bodies, exercising jurisdiction over their own lands and people. The United States Government has given repeated assurances that it would guarantee the survival of American Indians, their land base, and their tribal groups.

The ACLU recognizes that American Indians and their tribes, in addition to the constitutional rights to which all individuals are entitled, have rights recognized by treaties, compacts, and government commitments. The ACLU supports the rights of Indian peoples to:

1) A tribal land base and appurtenant natural resources;[1]

2) Tribal self government;

3) Retention of their cultural and religious heritage and

4) Enforcement of the commitments made to them by the United States in treaties, compacts, and by other governmental actions. [Board Minutes, December 7-8, 1974.]

[1] The reference to "appurtenant natural resources" is not meant to commit the Union to a broad policy of affirmative government action on economic issues affecting Indians. The reference is meant to apply, for example, to water rights, which are regarded as a central feature of the Indian land base.

Indian Civil Rights Act of 1968

The ACLU firmly supports the right of all individuals to be free from governmental abuse of power, whether the offending government be federal, state, or tribal. With respect to the latter government, however, the ACLU must remain sensitive to, and be prepared to defend, the needs of the tribe, which needs are expressed in the statement of general policy. Thoughtful investigation of the countervailing interests must precede any action which may affect basic tribal values and institutions.

Where action is deemed necessary, it should be taken first within the framework of tribal government, where an expeditious and effective tribal remedy is available. Provided that specific cases unique to Indian rights in which ACLU or its affiliates are asked to participate shall be presented to both Indian Rights Committee members and to the national legal director and general counsel for recommendations. However, this procedure is not intended to interfere with the right of each affiliate ultimately to make its own decision, within normal procedures, whether or not to engage in litigation. [Board Minutes, December 7-8, 1974, June 21-22, 1975.]

Welfare Programs

The ACLU is, in principle, sympathetic to federal or state welfare programs for American Indians, but it will extend support to specific programs only when civil liberties issues, rather than purely economic issues, are involved. One such issue is raised by the exclusion of Indians from state welfare programs, an exclusion that state officials may attempt to justify on a variety of technical legal grounds but that is often in reality a flagrant denial of equal protection of the law through racial discrimination. [Minutes of Indian Civil Rights Panel, January 10, 1958; ACLU amicus brief, *In re Beltrami vs. Minnesota,* 1961.] (See also policy on Poverty and Civil Liberties.)

Hunting and Fishing Rights

The ACLU is committed to the survival of American Indians as a native people. We recognize the great importance of hunting and fishing to the preservation of the Indian way of life. While the right of Indians to engage in hunting and fishing activities within their reservations free from outside interference has generally been recognized, the right of Indians to hunt and fish outside of their reservations has long been a subject of controversy. State authorities have repeatedly challenged the existence and scope of such off-reservation rights. Indians have suffered from arrests, harassment, threats, and outright violence in attempting to exercise their off-reservation fishing and hunting rights.

The ACLU will support the full exercise of the right of Indians to hunt and fish outside of reservations within the framework of the following principles:

1) We support the full exercise of Indian hunting and fishing rights whether they are established by treaty, executive order, compact or agreement, or whether they are based on aboriginal right.

2) We will insist that any interference with such right by state or federal governments on the ground of conservation or resource management be:

a) The minimum consistent with preservation of the resource;

b) Based on a fair and equitable apportionment of the resource between the Indian people and others, giving the broadest possible recognition to Indians' needs.

3) We will insist that, in managing fish and game resources which are subject to Indian hunting and fishing rights, all non-Indian governmental authorities give full recognition to the Indian interest in such resources and to the right of Indians to hunt and fish on and off the reservation subject to tribal regulation.

4) We will support Indian tribes in resisting federal, state, or private action which would have the effect of significantly diminishing fish or game resources within the reservation, or which would restrict Indian fishing or hunting activities within the reservation. [Board Minutes, October 2-3, 1976.]

Sex Discrimination

Policy #314

Equal Rights Amendment

The central concept of civil liberties is that all individuals have the fundamental right to be judged on the basis of their individual characteristics and capabilities, not the characteristics and capabilities that are supposedly shared by any group or class to which they might belong. This fundamental right is the premise of the Fourteenth Amendment to the United States Constitution, which guarantees the equal protection of the laws to all individuals.

The Fourteenth Amendment has proved an effective tool for combating discrimination against members of certain groups, notably racial minorities. However, the United States Supreme Court has not seen fit to use this tool to combat sex discrimination, i.e., discrimination against members of the class that includes the majority of Americans—women.

Though the Fourteenth Amendment covers all "persons," when it was adopted in 1868 women were not "persons" in the legal sense. The Supreme Court has interpreted the Fourteenth Amendment in light of conditions prevailing at the time of its adoption. The United States Court of Appeals for the Fifth Circuit in the 1965 *White v. Crook* case declared that the Fourteenth Amendment applies to women, but the decision never was challenged before the Supreme Court by the ACLU's opponents in the case.

Since the Fourteenth Amendment has been available to the Supreme Court for 102 years and still has not been applied against sex discrimination, the ACLU believes it is time to fashion a new method.[1] The new method should be designed specifically to end discrimination against women in order to reinforce the Fourteenth Amendment guarantee of equal protection to all persons.

The Equal Rights Amendment is such a method. It is needed to end gross inequities in our legal system and to complete the job of making women full citizens under the Constitution.

It is wrong to suggest that we should not act because passage of the Amendment would cause some uncertainty and require legislation and, possibly, litigation to clarify its specific meanings. The same could be said of every section of the Constitution.

It is wrong also to assume that passage of the Equal Rights Amendment will invalidate any of the necessary protections and benefits that have been extended to women by statute. Rather, analysis of state laws that apply exclusively to women does not establish that they protect women in any important way. In fact, these laws do not protect women in the one area applicable exclusively to women—maternity benefits and job security. They are ineffective in dealing with the exploitation of women who receive lower pay than men. Furthermore, they are used to discriminate against women in job and promotion opportunities.

As for the effective benefits that are now afforded women by statute, if the Amendment is ratified, these benefits can be extended equally to men rather than taken away from women.

Because of sex differentiation in the American legal system, the sex that has been permitted to wield the greater influence in formulating the law has used its power to entrench its position at the expense of the other sex. That is why the Equal Rights Amendment is essential now as a proclamation of the principle of full equality to all individuals. The entire democratic experiment rests on that principle. [Board Minutes, September 26-27, 1970; Press Release, October 2, 1970.]

The 1974 Biennial Conference endorses passage of the Equal Rights Amendment as a priority policy of the ACLU. The Union shall lend support to ERA ratification movements in each affiliate area where passage is pending to ensure the rapid ratification of this necessary human rights amendment. [Board Minutes, September 28-29, 1974.]

We believe it important that the Equal Rights Amendment should be ratified in accordance with procedures that have prevailed heretofore, that is, a

---

[1] On November 22, 1971, in the case of *Reed v. Reed*, the Supreme Court for the first time struck down a state statute on the ground that it unconstitutionally discriminated against women. However, the opinion was based on a narrow constitutional doctrine which allowed the Court to declare the statute "arbitrary" because it was "wholly unrelated to [its] objectives." It did not declare that sex, like race, is "a suspect classification." Under the *Reed* opinion women must continue to persuade the courts on a case by case basis that statutory sexual distinctions are arbitrary. [Press Release, November 22, 1971.]

state may not rescind once it has approved a constitutional amendment. This will not bind the ACLU to a policy position on legislation governing the process for adoption of future constitutional amendments. [Board Minutes, June 9, 1976.]

(See also policy on Constitutional Conventions.)

***

Further Information (not policy)

In 1973 the Supreme Court decided in *Frontiero v. Richardson* that statutes providing unequal fringe benefits for male and female members of the armed forces are unconstitutional because such disparity has no rational basis. The Court, however, has still not added sex to the group of classifications which are inherently suspect, in part because of the Court's feeling that this question is now before state legislatures considering the Equal Rights Amendment.

Therefore, while the Utah law setting different ages of majority for men and women (*Stanton v. Stanton*), and the Social Security Act's provision granting benefits to the widow of a wage earner who has primary responsibility for the care of a child but denying corresponding benefits to a widower (*Weinberger v. Wiesenfeld*), were unanimously declared unconstitutional in the 1974 term, the Court did not declare sex a suspect classification. Since 1974, the Court has persisted in its refusal to consider sex as a suspect classification, although it continues to strike down sexually discriminatory statutes. In *Craig v. Boren* (1976), the Court invalidated an Oklahoma statute which prohibited the sale of 3.2% beer to men under the age of 21 and women under the age of 18.

As of March 1978, 35 states have ratified the Equal Rights Amendment. In order for the amendment to become law, three of the remaining 15 states must ratify by 1979.

Policy #315

Employment and Education

(a) The ACLU endorses the principle that the Fifth and Fourteenth Amendments and the proposed Equal Rights Amendment to the United States Constitution should be read to guarantee to all persons equal treatment under the law without differentiations based on sex. The Union supports litigation to apply this principle for the purpose of eliminating discrimination based on sex in employment. Experience has shown that laws and administrative regulations which classify persons on the basis of sex *per se* regulate women to a "separate but not equal" status and are therefore inherently discriminatory.

The ACLU supports legislative action to combat discrimination in employment against women, and educational efforts to change discriminatory attitudes in men and in women, resulting from traditional sex role stereotyping.

The ACLU also supports the inclusion of "sex" in all civil rights legislation—federal, state, and local—such as has already been done in Title VII of the 1964 Civil Rights Act and in numerous state Fair Employment Practices Acts, and encourages prompt and effective enforcement of such provisions.

The Union further supports labor standards legislation in the states which protect all workers equally without distinction as to sex. It encourages all efforts to revise state labor standards legislation in order to provide adequate conditions of work, wages and hours, and protection of health of all workers.

In working to achieve these objectives, the Union recognizes there may be need for legislation that differentiates on the basis of characteristics which are unique to one sex, such as pregnancy. Such legislation, where appropriate and reasonable under the Fourteenth Amendment, is designed not to separate women as a class, but to recognize certain circumstances in which special protections are necessary to achieve true equality for women. In this sense differential legislation can best be described in terms of groupings of a functional nature (i.e., dependent children, pregnant women, etc.) or groups possessing specific characteristics at any given time (the poor, the economically exploited, etc.). [Board Minutes, December 5-6, 1970.]

***

(b) No institution of higher education which receives public funds or any governmental assistance, financial or otherwise, may deny equal application from men and women, nor administer separate admissions requirements for men and women, nor deny to either men or women, on grounds of sex, access to any educational programs or opportunity for teaching fellowships or government scholarships offered. [Board Minutes, December 5-6, 1970.]

***

(c) The ACLU will take specific action to insure that all discriminatory laws, regulations and policies applicable to women because of their marital status be abolished. Marital status should never be a factor for terminating employment or education, for awarding scholarships, or for determining pay.

The ACLU will take action to insure that governmental assistance, including social security, welfare, unemployment compensation, and FHA loans, shall never be awarded or denied on the basis of sex.

The ACLU will take action to insure that neither pregnancy nor motherhood should be a cause for involuntary termination of education or employment or denial of opportunity for education or employment, if the woman's ability to perform is not impaired. [Board Minutes, December 5-6, 1970.]

***

(d) As an application of Union policy on equal employment opportunity for women, the ACLU endorses measures which would remove those barriers that have traditionally disadvantaged women in seeking and engaging in employment. The institution of government supported voluntary child-care centers for children of working mothers would be a measure that would tend to eliminate one such barrier, provided however, that child care centers funded by tax monies, tax deductions or tax credits, must fit within ACLU church-state policy. [Board Minutes, December 4-5, 1971.] (See also policy on Federally-Funded, Religiously-Owned Child Care Facilities.)

***

Athletics

Segregation by sex, as by race, in education leads to inequality of treatment, in access to facilities and available resources. While equal access to school physical education and athletic programs is necessary for both sexes, full participation by women in sports may require separate women's and men's teams, but, in any event, requires access to compete for participation on integrated teams. [Board Minutes, September 24-25, 1977.]

***

Further Information (not policy)

Title IX of the Educational Amendments of 1972 prohibits, with some exceptions, sex discrimination in educational programs or activities which receive federal financial assistance. Regulations for the enforcement of Title IX were only adopted in June, 1975 and allow for a one to three year adjustment period for institutions to comply. Because of the failure of the Department of Health, Education and Welfare to process Title IX complaints and the weaknesses in some areas of the regulations, the effect of Title IX is not known.

The regulations and the legislative intent are very good on treatment of pregnant students and employees within educational institutions and on equal access to academic programs. The regulations are disappointing with respect to athletic programming and self evaluation and record keeping by institutions to determine and rectify past discriminatory practices.

Title VII of the 1964 Civil Rights Act offers the strongest protection against pregnancy discrimination. The EEOC guidelines enforcing Title VII states that "A written policy or practice which excludes from employment applicants or employees because of pregnancy is in prima facie violation of Title VII." Courts have given great deference to these guidelines in deciding that the following policies affecting pregnant women are violative of Title VII: termination; termination for refusal to take leave of absence; termination of unmarried and married employees with less than two years service; refusal to reemploy women granted maternity leave; denial of disability benefit for pregnancy; and refusal to hire and or promote because of pregnancy.

In the companion cases of *Cleveland Board of Education v. La Fleur* and *Cohen v. Chesterfield County School Board,* the Supreme Court in 1974 invalidated on constitutional grounds a school board policy requiring pregnant school teachers to take an involuntary unpaid leave of absence in their fifth month of pregnancy. Although this case was finally resolved on due process rather than sex discrimination-equal protection grounds its practical effect was to bring a virtual halt to employers' efforts to vindicate mandatory unpaid leave policies for pregnant employees.

In 1975 the Supreme Court held that the Utah law declaring pregnant women ineligible to receive unemployment benefits for a period extending from 12 weeks before to six weeks after child birth was constitutionally invalid under the principles of the *La Fleur* decision. However, during the last few years, the Supreme Court has firmly rejected the idea that discrimination against pregnant women is sex discrimination and thus violative of the equal protection clause. In *Geduldig v. Aiello* (1974), the Court held that California's disability insurance system for private employees temporarily unable to work because of an injury or illness was not violative of the equal protection clause even though pregnancy was not included as a temporary disability. In *General Electric Company v. Gilbert* (1976), the Court held that a disability plan which excluded pregnancy from its definition of disabilities was not violative of Title VII of the Civil Rights Act of 1964 because the exclusion was "not gender-based discrimination" and because pregnancy is now "a voluntarily undertaken and desired condition." There is now federal legislation under consideration which will prohibit the exemption of pregnancy from employment disability plans.

During the last few years, there have been two other major Supreme Court decisions concerning sex discrimination in employment. In *Schlesinger v. Ballard* (1975), the Supreme Court upheld the Navy's "up or out" statute, under which male officers were mandatorily discharged when twice passed over for promotion while female officers were discharged only after they had been employed for a period of 13 years without promotion. The Court justified the use of an explicitly sex-based classification on the grounds that it supposedly compensated Navy women for other disadvantages which they experienced in the Navy, and that it insured the proper rate and flow of promotions. And, in *Dothord v. Rawlingson* (1977), the Court held that being male is an advantageous occupational qualification for the job of prison guard in a "contact" position in an Alabama male maximum security prison. The Court found that a female employee's "very womanhood" would undermine her capacity to provide the security that is the essence of a prison guard's job.

The Supreme Court has been extremely weak with respect to the issue of providing equal government benefits for men and women. In *Kahn v. Shevin* (1974), the Court upheld a Florida statute that granted only widows, and not widowers, an annual $500.00 property tax exemption. In *Califano v. Webster* (1977), a closely divided Supreme Court held valid a Social Security Act provision which gave uniformly higher old-age benefits to retired female wage earners but not to male wage earners who were similarly situated. But, in *Califano v. Goldfarb*, a similarly divided Court held unconstitutional a Social Security Act provision which gave survivors' benefits to a widower only if he could prove that he had been receiving at least half of his support from his deceased wife while automatically giving a widow such benefits regardless of whether she had actually been dependent on her deceased husband.

In *Vorcheimer v. School District of Philadelphia* (1977), the Supreme Court held that the Philadelphia school district's maintenance of two sexually segregated senior high schools for scholastically distinguished students, in an other wise co-educational system, was constitutionally permissible.

Policy #316

ACLU Internal Organization

(a) The ACLU has stood for equal rights for all persons without discrimination based on sex. Inspite of this enlightened policy, the ACLU in its own practices has underutilized the potentialities and talents of women in the organization. Although the ACLU has made continuing efforts to implement its policy of sexual equality, the organization has not taken sufficient notice of the fact that the womens' rights movement has escalated to the point where it must now be considered high priority. The ACLU will respond with greater speed and intensity in this growing crisis as it has to other emergency situations which involve infringements on basic civil liberties.

Therefore, the ACLU will implement the following policies.

1) The ACLU will take affirmative and vigorous action within its own structures—national and affiliate—to increase significantly the representation of women on all policy-making bodies and committees of the organization. Token representation will no longer be acceptable. (See also policy on Internal Employment)

2) Parallel efforts will be made to open up to women all executive and policy-making staff positions, including the executive directorship of the national office. Equal pay for equal work will be applied. [Board Minutes, December 5-6, 1970.]

***

(b) The ACLU Constitution shall be amended to provide for six additional at-large members of the national Board of Directors, bringing the total of such Directorships to thirty-six. The six additional seats are to be filled at the at-large election following the constitutional change and are to be staggered for one, two and three year terms. The Board will direct the Nominating Committee in developing the slate for such election to give the ACLU electorate an opportunity to fill the additional seats with women not presently incumbents on the Board.

In anticipation of increased representation of women on the national Board, it is reasonable to expect increased representation of women on the national Executive Committee and among the national officers. The Board shall direct the Special Nominating Committee to place women candidates on the slates for the national Executive Committee and national officerships.

The Constitution of the ACLU authorizes the chairperson of the national Board, with the Board's advice and consent, to appoint the chairpersons and members of ACLU structural committees (other than the Executive Committee). Membership on the structural committees of the ACLU reflects the composition of the national Board. Because of the low representation of women on the national Board, any plan to increase significantly their representation on these committees would require the same women to carry several assignments. The chairperson of the Board and the chairpersons of the committees should be directed to review all committee structures with a view toward the goal of increasing participation of women as rapidly as circumstances permit. Wherever possible, women members of the ACLU who are not presently Board members should be invited to serve on these committees.

The Constitution of the ACLU authorizes the chairperson of the national Board, with the Board's advice and consent, to appoint the chairpersons and members of ACLU subject matter committees. Women presently represent *in toto* 24 percent of the subject-matter committees, reflecting greater progress toward participation than in other structures of the ACLU. It is recognized that continuous service on these committees is influenced in large part by geographical considerations—the nearness of residence to the New York metropolitan area. Within this limitation, however, the chairperson of the Board and the chairpersons of the various committees are requested to review their committee structures, to institute affirmative action to increase significantly participation of women in the committees and to encourage the election of women to the chairpersonship of such committees. Chairpersons will also be requested to report annually to the national Board, through the Women's Rights Steering Committee, the results of their efforts.

The Women's Rights Steering Committee shall be enlarged and shall have the following functions:

1) To examine the participation of women in national and affiliate staff positions, and in other activities not covered by this statement, and to report to the national Board by June 1, 1973 with specific recommendations for an affirmative action plan, or other remedial measures, to the extent the Committee deems necessary.

2) To cooperate with the national staff to devise an affirmative action program to enlarge the membership of women in the ACLU nationwide.

3) To review annual Womens' Rights Audits from the national ACLU and the affiliates and to report and make recommendations to the national Board for actions the Committee deems necessary to further implement this policy.

Based upon observation of the makeup of the affiliate representation on the national Board and the proportionate inequality of participation of women in the policy-making activities of the affiliates as reflected in the Womens' Rights Audit, the national Board calls upon each affiliate to examine the present participation of women in its structure at all levels, including any existing affirmative action program and representation of women on the national Board of Directors, and to adopt an affirmative remedial program to redress any existing inequities. The affiliate is requested to submit to the national office by no later than June 1, 1973 the results of its appraisal and program it has adopted.

The reports and programs shall be reviewed by the Womens' Rights Steering Committee. If an affiliate fails to submit a proposal or its proposal is deemed unsatisfactory, the Womens' Rights Steering Committee shall propose to the Board an affirmative action program which, if adopted by the Board, the affiliate shall be called upon to execute.

Each affiliate shall annually, by no later than June 1, report on compliance with and effectiveness of any affirmative action program it has adopted or been called upon to execute and submit an annual audit on womens' rights to the Womens' Rights Steering Committee.

The national Board shall delegate to the Womens' Rights Steering Committee the responsibility for monitoring compliance by affiliates. The Womens' Rights Steering Committee shall review the affiliates' annual reports and make specific recommendations to the national Board in any instance where it deems action to be necessary.

Each affiliate which has not yet established a Women's Rights Committee is hereby urged to do so. Such affiliate committee should have functions which include: 1) appraising the participation of women at all levels of staff and lay governance; 2) assisting the affiliate in preparing the annual Womens' Rights Audit; 3) developing and maintaining liaison with the national Womens' Rights Steering Committee; 4) assisting the affiliate in developing programs to enlarge the membership of women in the affiliate and its chapters; 5) assisting the affiliate in increasing equal opportunities for the employment of women at all staff levels; 6) such other functions as the affiliate deems appropriate for the implementation of this policy.

The national Board strongly recommends that each affiliate adopt as its affirmative goal the reconstitution of its affiliate board over a three-year period so that the percentage of women board members approximates at least the percentage of women members of the affiliate. [Board Minutes, February 17-18, 1973.]

***

(c) After receiving in 1975 a report from the Womens' Rights Steering Committee that compliance with the Board's 1973 resolutions had generally been satisfactory, the Board adopted the following measures:

1) Urging all affiliates to continue to implement affirmative action plans in order to achieve in fact, as well as spirit, the goals of the Board's 1973 resolutions.

2) Urging the 1975 Nominating Committee to be especially sensitive to the need to present to the electorate a slate with a large number of women nominees.

3) Urging the Womens' Rights Steering Committee, in the spirit of the 1973

Board resolutions, to continue its program of reviewing national and affiliate performance, including the important area of employment practices. The national office should maintain the present level of staffing of the Women's Rights Steering Committee. [Board Minutes, February 15-16, 1975.]

The inability of some affiliates to reach their goals has been due to lack of resources rather than will. Greater involvement in specific womens' rights issues will bring more women into greater general participation within the ACLU. The national office, through the Womens' Rights Project and the Development Department, should utilize national resources in such a way as to increase affiliate programmatic activity. [Board Minutes, September 27-28, 1975.]

***

(d) After receiving reports that several candidates for affiliate employment have been interviewed concerning child care responsibilities, husband's employment and other prohibited matters, the Board adopted the position that affiliates should be instructed by the national office that such interviewing is both a violation of Title VII of the 1964 Civil Rights Act and totally inconsistent with ACLU policy.

***

(e) In 1977 the Board adopted the following resolution recommended by the 1976 Biennial Conference: The Women's Rights Project is commended for its current litigative efforts as outlined in the papers prepared for the 1976 Biennial Conference. In addition, the National Board is urged to expand its policies in the women's rights area to cover whatever educational, legislative or litigative efforts may be found necessary to enhance the rights of working women, gay women, and abused women. [Board Minutes, March 5-6, 1977.]

Policy #317

Poverty and Civil Liberties

General Policy

Poverty as we now know it is largely, if only partially, a result of denials throughout this country's history of equal treatment because of race, sex, ethnic background, religion, and physical defect or condition. Poverty cannot be explained as resulting from "natural" economic differences.

Poverty today is concentrated disproportionately among racial and ethnic minorities. The effects of the segregation of poor people in urban ghettos, which are inadequately supplied with housing, educational, and health facilities and municipal services, has long been a civil liberties concern. Similarly, the frequent denials of civil liberties to which poor people are subjected because of their economic dependence on government has also been a civil liberties concern.

The failure of society fully to solve the problems of poverty inevitably results in continued subjugation of the poor to violations of their civil liberties and civil rights, out of proportion to their numbers. The poor are denied due process, the right of privacy, the equal protection of the laws, and other constitutional guarantees far more seriously and far more frequently than the middle class and the wealthy.

Furthermore, when there is a direct and substantial connection between poverty and *particular* deprivations of civil liberties and civil rights, the ACLU will support positive governmental action to mitigate the effects of poverty so as to eliminate or curtail the particular deprivations of civil liberties and civil rights. [Board Minutes, June 16-17, 1973; December 3-4, 1977.]

The ACLU and its affiliates recognize and urge that the denial of benefits necessary to the basic sustenance of life of some persons, while comparable benefits are afforded by government to others, has constitutional significance insofar as the requirements of equal protection and due process are concerned.[1]

The constitutional significance of such benefits is that equal protection prohibits the exclusion of some people just because of "some reason" or a "minimum reason." Both legislatures *and* the courts must be convinced that the reasons for the exclusion of some persons have been carefully and strictly scrutinized, and are compelling. Put another way, classifications which exclude some people from the basic necessities of life, while granting such necessities to others, are constitutionally "suspect." The ACLU rejects the analysis as well as the holding of the Supreme Court in *Dandridge v. Williams* (1970).[1]

In light of the drastic cutbacks in governmental benefit programs currently underway, as well as the inadequate legislative-judicial response to equal protection and due process issues in social welfare programs, the ACLU and its affiliates will themselves evaluate whether compelling societal reasons exist for exclusion of persons from major governmental programs involving basic necessities of life. Where the ACLU and/or its affiliate concludes that no such compelling reason exists, the Union and/or affiliate will actively advocate, in both court and legislature, against such exclusion.

The national Board should appoint a committee to develop and report upon the more detailed contours of such a policy for action purposes. [Board Minutes, December 3-4, 1977.]

[1]*Dandridge v. Williams* (1970) rejected the view that equal protection requires strict judicial scrutiny and a showing of compelling societal interests where governmental programs excluded some persons in need while granting basic necessities of life to others. In *Memorial Hospital v. Maricopa County* (1974), however, the Supreme Court concluded that:

"... it is at least clear that medical care is as much 'a basic necessity of life' to an indigent as welfare assistance. And, governmental privileges or benefits necessary to basic sustenance have often been viewed as being of greater constitutional significance than less essential forms of government entitlement."

The cases to which the latter conclusion has been applied are limited to those involving certain aspects of procedure or such other constitutional rights as travel. *Memorial Hospital* does not repudiate the Dandridge analysis, as urged in the resolution.

Health Care

There has been a massive growth of government intervention and support of health care delivery, medical research and education, and hospital construction. Such government intervention raises traditional civil liberties problems such as lack of due process, unequal treatment and invasion of privacy. Congress is now debating a series of bills involving even more massive government sponsorship of health care programs. Therefore, the ACLU should take positive steps in the legal, legislative and educational fields to ensure that governmental action in the health field conforms with traditional areas of civil liberties concerns, and provides fair and equal access to adequate medical care.[1] [Board Minutes, September 28-29, 1974.]

Welfare Recipients

(a) The ACLU strongly opposes the many aspects of our welfare system that violate basic concerns of fairness, dignity, and privacy that are part of the fabric of civil liberties. To be poor is tragedy enough. To be forced to forego elementary rights of privacy and decency in order to obtain financial assistance is improper and violates the fundamental precepts of a democratic society.

The ACLU therefore will, among other efforts, support legislation, litigation, and educational programs to protect: (1) the right of privacy of the poor, by opposing such tactics as midnight visits to the homes of those receiving assistance, and by supporting the right of recipients of assistance to bar caseworkers from their homes (unless authorized by a search warrant) without fear of losing governmental assistance; (2) the right to a hearing, with counsel if desired, for welfare applicants and recipients in connection with their right to assistance or respecting the reduction or termination of assistance; (3) the right to travel freely and to live where they wish in accordance with their means, by opposing unreasonable state and local residence requirements or laws permitting the exiling of the poor to their previous state of residence.

The ACLU further believes that our welfare system should be analyzed to determine whether previous abuses of the types described above, or other types, may be eliminated or reduced by new approaches designed to eliminate the kinds of situations which engender the abuses. Thus, the substitution, where possible, of visits by recipients to the office of the caseworker in place of the latter's visits to the home may help eliminate the invasion of privacy to which many needy are subjected. The opportunity for a hearing on rejected claims for assistance (with counsel, if desired) should be guaranteed by governmental agencies. Information as to the right to a hearing should be automatically distributed with the rejection notice itself. [Board Minutes, October 4-5, 1969.]

***

(b) Although the Union does not oppose, in principle, requirements that

---

[1] This policy is not intended to assert that government is required, as a matter of civil liberties concern, to provide adequate medical care. It is merely intended to assert that when government does provide medical care, it must do so on a basis of fair and equal access for all.

welfare recipients work at legally assigned tasks to maintain their eligibility for relief payments, it holds that criminal prosecution and imprisonment for refusal to accept such tasks amounts to involuntary servitude and is prohibited by the Thirteenth Amendment. The maximum penalty for refusal to work should be ineligibility for further relief. [News Release, January 8, 1964.] POLICY UNDER REVIEW.

***

(c) If a government grants a welfare benefit to a class of citizens, the principles of due process and equal protection of the laws forbid the withholding of benefits from some members of that class unless there is a logical and reasonable basis for classification. For example, a state Aid to Dependent Children program may not withhold payments for the support of a child whose mother bears illegitimate children while she is on welfare, because illegitimacy is an irrelevant classification which does not justify denial of assistance to admittedly needy children. (The Supreme Court has upheld the Union's view with regard to denial both for reasons of illegitimacy and for failure to complete residency requirements.) Further, such a statute, while not discriminatory on its face, may well be designed to deprive a single class of citizens of their rights in a roundabout attempt to approximate a racial classification and thus circumvent the Supreme Court's precedent-making decision (in the 1954 segregation case) that a racial classification *per se* is not a reasonable one. [News Release, November 29, 1960.] (See also policy on Federal Benefits and Loyalty Tests.)

***

(d) The Union opposes government restrictions on the use of federal funds in anti-poverty birth control programs administered through the Office of Economic Opportunity. The specific restrictions are prohibitions on the distribution of funds for contraceptive aid to unmarried women or women living apart from their husbands, for announcing or promoting through the mass media family planning program information, and for voluntary sterilization. All three violate the constitutional guarantee of equal protection of the laws.

The Fifth Amendment guarantee of due process, embracing the concept of equal protection of the laws, means that in the disposing of government funds no distinctions unrelated to the purpose of a legislative act can be drawn among the class of citizens who are beneficiaries of the government's aid. Thus, a criterion barring aid to women who are unmarried or living apart from their husbands is unrelated to the purpose of an act designed to relieve poverty.

Equal treatment with respect to birth control aid is especially important because persons in higher income groups, married and unmarried alike, have access to medical contraceptive guidance by virtue of being able to afford private medical consultation. But the poor, who are the concern of the program, have no such access. In view of this fact, and of the apparent high rate of illegitimacy in the low-income group, it seems clear that unmarried women or women living apart from their husbands have a need for birth control guidance that is at least equal to that of similarly situated women in higher-income groups.

Further discrimination against the poverty group is involved in the OEO's guideline denying funds for voluntary sterilization. This denial, when such treatment is indicated for health reasons and when the patient is made fully aware of the implications, cannot be justified in view of the ease with which a wealthy person can obtain this treatment privately. The Union's position on this matter follows in the path of actions taken in other areas to assure that the concept of equal treatment applies to poor persons. For example, poor persons may not be disadvantaged in criminal trials, and it is a violation of due process for the government to deny counsel or the effective right of appeal to those who cannot afford these essential aids to legal defense.

Challenging the OEO's prohibition of use of funds for promotion through the mass media, the Union points out that administrative action on the part of a government agency that intentionally restricts dissemination of information to the public could amount to censorship. The freedom of information problem is intensified by overtones of unequal protection of the laws, for experience has clearly demonstrated that poor persons do not have equal opportunity to obtain facts concerning birth control and need these facts at least as much as persons of means. It seems both fair and logical that the means of communication most accessible to the poor, the mass media, should not be barred from transmitting information as to the availability of family planning programs financed by OEO grants. [Board Minutes, February 14, 1966; News Release, March 30, 1966.] (See also policy on Right of Choice in Family Planning.)

Policy #319

Residency Requirements for Recipients of Government Benefits

Residency requirements, whether previous, durational, present or continuing, and whether interstate or intrastate, which are maintained as a condition of receiving a government-related right or benefit, constitute a violation of civil liberties, unless the residency requirement is supported by a compelling government interest directly related to the right or benefit conferred.

The following definitions should apply:

1) *Previous Residency Requirement:* A residency requirement conditioning the receipt of a right or benefit upon a person having been a resident of the state at some particular time in the past. For example, to be eligible for the New York State veterans' preference, an individual must have been a resident of New York at the time of his or her induction. N.Y. Civ. Serv. Law §85 (1) (a) McKinney 1973).

2) *Durational Residency Requirement:* This requires that a person reside within the state or other political subdivision for a specified time period before becoming eligible to receive a government benefit.

3) *Present Residency Requirement:* This requires that the individual be a resident of the state or political subdivision at the time he or she seems a particular government right or benefit.

4) *Continuing Residency Requirement:* This conditions the continued receipt of a right or benefit upon remaining a resident of the state or political subdivision.

Examples of those few circumstances where residency requirements would be permissible include:

a) Durational (not longer than 30 days for administrative purposes), present, and continuing residency requirements for voting. These residency requirements for voting would allow a jurisdiction to be assured that its officials were elected by and responsive to its own residents, and would serve to prevent duplicative voting.

b) Present and continuing residency requirements for municipal employment where such requirements would help to effectuate an affirmative action employment policy and would assure employment opportunities for persons best acquainted with municipal problems. These residency requirements, as noted, would be permissible when used by a jurisdiction to compensate for past practices of discrimination, and to hire as employees those persons who are or would become personally familiar with the jurisdiction's problems. A reasonable period of adjustment should be provided if such policies are adopted.

c) Present and continuing residency requirements for such rights and benefits as lower tuition at educational institutions. These residency requirements would permit use of a jurisdiction's limited financial resources for those people who do or might in the future contribute to those resources.

d) Present residency but not durational requirements for such rights and benefits as public assistance (welfare).

In each of the above instances, the governmental interests would appear to satisfy the substantial and compelling government interest directly related to the right or benefit conferred test.

In most instances, however, residency requirements would not be permissible since they are not supportable by a substantial and compelling government interest directly related to the right or benefit conferred. Examples include: residency requirements for professional licensing since competency examinations, not residency, properly serve the governmental interest in licensing competent professionals; most or all forms of durational residency requirements (e.g., for welfare, lower tuition, employment), except for necessary administrative purposes, since durational status is seldom if ever related to any right or benefit; and previous residency, or any other residency requirement, for federal veteran benefits or preferences since military service, not residency, relates to the governmental interest in rewarding veterans who served their country.

As stated at the outset, residency requirements constitute a violation of civil liberties; this presumption may be rebutted, but only where the residency requirement is supported by a compelling government interest directly related to the right or benefit conferred. [Board Minutes, March 5-6, 1977.]

(See also policies on Poverty and Civil Liberties, Education, and Voting Rights.)

Immigration and Naturalization

Policy #323

Admission of Immigrants

Whatever method Congress may choose to select immigrants for admission to the United States, ancestry, color, nationality (whether defined in terms of a nation, colony or dependency) sex, religion or race should not be the basis for exclusion. The ACLU favors elimination from the existing immigration laws of all vestigial remains of the now-repealed national origins quota system, including the maintenance of subquotas for colonies and dependent areas of foreign states.

Aliens should not be barred from admission to the United States as permanent residents upon grounds relating to their beliefs or advocacy of any ideas, including political doctrine.

Aliens should not be barred from admission to the United States as permanent residents upon grounds which are vague or subject to the arbitrary exercise of discretion.

Aliens should not be barred from admission to the United States as permanent residents upon grounds not reasonably related to any proper governmental concern.[1]

The historic tradition of asylum should be established as a settled tenet of American immigration policy. The right of asylum should be made available to persons who are in danger of persecution for reasons of political beliefs, religious persuasion or ethnic, national or racial origins.[2]

---

[1] For instance, ACLU policy on Homosexuality makes the following specific reference to aliens:

"Just as governmental discrimination by race, alienage, religion or sex is a denial of equal protection, so, too, is governmental discrimination on the basis of sexual or affectional preference. Homosexuality per se implies no disability that would justify such discrimination. The ACLU opposes the exclusion, deportation and refusal to naturalize homosexual aliens."

[2] ACLU policy on ACLU's Role in International Civil Liberties Matters includes the following support of the right of political asylum:

"The ACLU will aid persons from foreign lands to secure political asylum in the United States when these persons seek refuge from persecution for their political, religious or other beliefs or associations."

This passage is incorporated into our review of ACLU immigration policies because of the interrelationship of immigration and international civil liberties issues.

Any alien outside the United States who is denied a visa, or refused admission to the United States as an immigrant should have the right to an adjudicatory proceeding, which shall include the right of representation, to present evidence, to examine and to object to evidence against the applicant, a written record of the proceedings, and the decision by the adjudicating officer based upon the evidence in the record.

Any alien who is denied a visa by the adjudicating officer in an administrative proceeding shall be entitled to the same rights of judicial review as is enjoyed by aliens within the United States. [Board Minutes, June 18-19, 1977.]

Policy #324

Admission of Non-Immigrants

Aliens who are otherwise eligible to obtain visitors' visas should not be barred from admission to the United States because of their ancestry, color, nationality, sex, religion, race, or sexual or affectional preference, upon grounds relating to their beliefs or advocacy of any ideas, including political doctrine, or upon grounds which are vague or which are subject to the arbitrary exercise of discretion. Nor should the grant or maintenance of non-immigrant status by students, business visitors, visitors for pleasure or any other non-immigrants be denied by reason of the exercise of the constitutional right of free speech or association or membership in any party, or conditioned upon the limitation of the right to travel within the United States.

Aliens who have been denied visas to enter the United States should have the right to have the consular decision reviewed in an administrative proceeding and be entitled to the same right of judicial review which is afforded to other persons who are aggrieved by governmental action. [Board Minutes, September 24-25, 1977.]

Policy #325

Naturalization

The naturalization envisioned by the Constitution is one which, when achieved for the naturalized citizen, places that citizen upon an equal footing with the native born citizen of the United States. As Congress would have no power to impose conditions on the retention of citizenship by naturalized citizens, the conditions which it would impose on the grant of citizenship should be reasonably limited to those requirements which indicate an identity with the people of the United States.

The ACLU opposes any conditions upon the grant of citizenship which would bar persons because of their political beliefs, other than an allegiance to a foreign state, or a standard of conduct which would not debar a natural citizen of the United States from the exercise of his rights of citizenship. Such standards, where applicable, should be applied through a process of judicial inclusion and exclusion, permitting naturalization to be determined through an adjudicatory method reflecting prevailing standards of conduct rather than by rigid legislative definition. [Board Minutes, September 24-25, 1977.]

Policy #326

Loss of Citizenship

An American citizen has the right to expatriate himself or herself voluntarily and to achieve the status of an alien in respect to the United States government. [Board Minutes, August 19, 1968.]

The ACLU believes that Congress should be without power to deprive a native-born or naturalized citizen of the United States of citizenship in the absence of an international and voluntary renunciation of allegiance except in those cases in which a naturalized citizen has acquired citizenship by a willful misrepresentation or concealment of a fact material to his eligibility to citizenship. Any proceeding to denaturalize a naturalized citizen upon such grounds should be subject to a statute of limitations of 10 years.

Where Congress has conferred citizenship at birth to persons born outside of the United States of any parent who is a citizen of the United States, such "statutory citizens at birth" should be afforded the same right to citizenship which is afforded to native-born and to naturalized citizens. Their citizenship should not be divested except upon their intentional and voluntary renunciation of allegiance. [Board Minutes, September 24-25, 1977.]

Aliens

Policy #327

Employment of Undocumented Aliens

The ACLU remains opposed to legislation which penalizes employers for hiring aliens unlawfully in the United States. We believe that such legislation would exacerbate existing patterns of racial and ethnic discrimination in employment, by creating greater risks for employers hiring applicants whom they believe to be aliens. (See also policy on Property Ownership.)

The ACLU also opposes the use of Social Security cards and other governmentally-issued documents as a condition of employment. Such a practice, in effect, creates an "employment passport," which results in a universal identifier of all persons in the United States. [Board Minutes, June 18-19, 1977.]

Policy #328

Detention and Registration

The ACLU opposes the enactment of alien registration laws, which treat the alien population as a separate and quasi-criminal element of society and create an easy avenue for surveillance of those who hold unpopular beliefs. [Board Minutes, July 24, 1939; Minutes of Executive Committee, January 11, 1926; Weekly Bulletin, March 31, 1926.]

The Union did not take a stand against the principle of detention of enemy aliens in this country during World War II, although on numerous occasions it did protest specific injustices in the administration of the program. In 1942, and twice in 1944, however, the ACLU challenged judicially the restriction and detention by military authorities of civilian citizens without any regard for the requirements of due process (pressing of specific charges, proper hearing, etc.) and without any proof of justification by reasons of national security in wartime. The subjects of these detention measures were the victims of blatant racial discrimination because they were not enemy aliens at all, but native-born Americans of Japanese ancestry, and thus were denied equal protection of the law in being singled out for evacuation and resettlement for no apparent reason other than their race. [*Annual Reports* and Board Minutes, 1941-1944; ACLU amicus briefs, *Hirabayashi vs. USA*, 1942, *Korematsu vs. U.S.*, 1944, *Endo vs. Eisenhower*, 1944.]

Policy #329

Deportation

(a) Deportation from the United States is a punishment which cannot be constitutionally imposed upon its citizens. The ACLU believes that it is at all times a denial of due process to inflict upon a lawful permanent resident alien punishment which cannot be imposed upon a citizen of the United States who has engaged in the identical conduct, and it may, in particular circumstances, be cruel and unusual punishment. For persons who have become absorbed into the American community, living and working in the United States as full members of its society deportation cannot be and should not be regarded as the exercise of any "foreign policy" of the United States government.

***

(b) Although aliens who have acquired their status as permanent residents by fraud or otherwise illegally may, without offending due process, be subject to deportation, the ACLU favors in this area, as in other offenses against the government, a statute of limitations barring deportation for any fraudulent or illegal entry to the United States which has occurred. Nor does the ACLU believe that deportation should be inflicted upon those under the age of eighteen who may have been admitted to the United States for permanent residence as the result of an illegal or fraudulent act. [Board Minutes, June 18-19, 1977.]

***

(c) Where relief is afforded from deportation by reasons of hardship or other factors, such benefits should be granted without discrimination to persons from any country and to persons regardless of their occupation or method of admission to the United States. Neither should any person who has been granted relief from deportation be debarred from any rights or benefits which are otherwise available to persons in the U.S. under the Immigration law and other statutes and the Constitution of the U.S. Nor should any person who is deportable from the United States be deported to a country where he has had no prior residence or to a country where he will be subject to persecution. [Board Minutes, September 24-25, 1977.]

ORGANIZATIONAL POLICIES

Policy #501

Constitution

(Adopted January 7, 1957, after Corporation vote, with amendments as of December 1976.)

SECTION 1. *Name*

The name of this membership corporation, as stated in the certificate of incorporation, is "American Civil Liberties Union, Inc."

SECTION 2. *Objects*

The objects of the American Civil Liberties Union shall be to maintain and advance civil liberties, including the freedoms of association, press, religion, and speech, and the rights to the franchise, to due process of law, and to equal protection of the laws for all people throughout the United States and its possessions. The Union's objects shall be sought wholly without political partisanship.

SECTION 3. *Headquarters*

The Union's national headquarters shall be located as determined by its national Board of Directors.

SECTION 4. *Management*

The management of the Union's business shall be vested in its national Board of Directors, as hereinafter provided.

SECTION 5. *Membership*

(A) A member of the Union shall be a person or organization paying such membership dues as may be prescribed from time to time by the national Board of Directors.

(B) A member may be suspended or removed from the Union, or a prospective member may be excluded—after hearing, if he or she so desires—by vote of a majority of the actual membership of the national Board of Directors.

SECTION 6. *Affiliates*

(A) Any group of persons residing in the United States or its possessions may apply for recognition as an affiliate of the Union, and the national Board of Directors shall so recognize the group when satisfied that the purposes of the Union will be so served. An affiliate shall act in accordance with the policies of the Union, with the understanding that the purposes of this requirement is to obtain general unity rather than absolute uniformity.

(B) The structure and functioning of an affiliate, including its relations with the national organization and with its own chapters (if any), shall be governed by rules adopted form time to time by the national Board of Directors, subject to the recommendations of the Biennial Conference.

(C) An affiliate may be suspended or removed from the Union—after hearing, if the affiliate so desires—by vote of two-thirds of the actual membership of the national Board of Directors.

SECTION 7. *Governing Bodies*

(A) The board of an affiliate shall be composed of persons who are members of that affiliate, and shall be electorally responsible to the affiliate's membership. To establish such electoral responsibility, the affiliate's constitution or by-laws shall provide that:

1) Election of its board members shall be for reasonable terms and in a manner by which all the affiliate's members have reasonable opportunity to vote, as by a ballot mailed to each. If the board members are delegates from chapters, they shall be reasonably apportioned to the geographical distribution of the affiliate's membership; and, if they are elected indirectly by chapter boards, those chapter boards shall be electorally responsible to their respective chapter memberships.

2) Reasonable opportunity shall be afforded the affiliate's (or chapter's) membership to nominate candidates for the affiliate (or chapter) board, and to initiate amendments to the affiliate (or chapter) constitution and by-laws. Any vacancy in an affiliate (or chapter) board existing between regular elections may be filled by the board of the affiliate (or chapter).

(B) The number of members of the National Advisory Council shall be determined by the Board of Directors. Each member of the National Advisory Council shall be a member of the Union (apportioned roughly according to the population of the main geographical sections of the United States and its possessions, and selected to obtain the widest possible distribution of support of persons currently active publicly in behalf of civil liberties—if possible, to the extent of being readily recognized nationally), and approximately one-third of that authorized membership shall be elected each year for three-year terms in the following manner:

1) Nominations shall be made by the Nominating Committee hereinafter provided for, after seeking suggestions from all members of the Union. Further nominations may be made by petition of any five members of the national Board of Directors, any ten members of the National Advisory Council, the boards of any three affiliates, or any fifty members of the Union.

2) Election shall be by a majority of the total membership of the Board of Directors, voting by mail ballot if necessary.

Any vacancy in the National Advisory Council existing between annual elections may be filled by the national Board of Directors for the remainder of its term.

(C) The national Board of Directors shall be composed of the following persons, each of whom shall be a member of the Union, (a) one director elected by each affiliate, (b) thirty-six directors who shall be elected at-large, and (c) the Chairman of the National Advisory Council *ex officio*. Provided, however, that after the election of thirty-six members at large, any vacancy caused by natural attrition shall not be filled until the Board returns to thirty members at-large.[1]

1) The affiliate directors on the national Board shall be elected by their respective affiliate boards. The at-large members of the national Board shall be elected in the following manner:

(i) Nominations shall be made by the Nominating Committee hereinafter provided for, after seeking suggestions from all members of the Union. The Nominating Committee shall circulate its list of nominees for the national Board at least four weeks prior to the closing date for nominations by petition. Further nominations may be made by petition of any five members of the national Board of Directors, any ten members of the National Advisory Council, the boards of any three affiliates, or any fifty members of the Union.

(ii) The electors shall be the following persons, voting by mail:

(a) The members of the boards of the affiliates, voting individually and each casting as many votes as there are members of his or her affiliate divided by that affiliate's actual board membership, and

(b) The members of the national Board of Directors, voting individually and each casting as many votes as one-third of the membership of the Union divided by the actual membership of the national Board of Directors, provided that a member of the national Board of Directors who is also a member of an affiliate board may choose in which capacity to vote, but shall not vote in more than one capacity.

2) Except for the Chairman of the National Advisory Council, who shall serve during his or her term of office, the terms of all members of the national Board shall be three years, but no more than one-third of the at-large members, exclusive of vacancies, shall be elected in any one year. The terms of the members of the national Board shall expire on June 30th.

3) No person who is a paid employee of the Union, or any of its affiliates, subsidiaries, or related bodies, shall be eligible to be a candidate for or to serve as a member of the national Board.

(D) The Executive Committee shall be composed of the chairman of the corporation and ten additional members of the national Board.

1) Nominations for membership on the Executive Committee shall be made by a special nominating committee of not less than three and not more than five members of the national Board, appointed by the chairman of the corporation, with the advice and consent of the Board. The report of the special nominating committee shall be distributed within a reasonable period prior to the meeting at which the election of the Executive Committee is to be held. Additional nominations may be made by any member of the Board.

---

[1] By a resolution of the Board of Directors adopted at its September 29-30, 1973 meeting natural attrition in Section 7(C) shall be defined as death or resignation during a Board member's term, or the declination by an incumbent Board member to have his or her name presented to the Nominating Committee for consideration.

2) The election of the members of the Executive Committee shall be held at a regular meeting of the national Board. The members shall be elected under a method of preferential voting to be selected by the Board. The terms of all Executive Committee members shall be two years. No more than five members, exclusive of vacancies, shall be elected in any year. The general counsel of the Union, if not elected members of the Executive Committee, shall be *ex officio* members, without vote. The executive director, any staff member whom he or she designates, shall attend and shall be permitted to participate in the meetings of the Executive Committee.

Any vacancy in the Executive Committee arising between annual elections may be filled at a regular meeting of the national Board by a majority vote of those present; if no majority is obtained, a run-off election shall be held. Any person so elected will hold office only until the next annual election.

3) The Executive Committee may exercise the powers vested in the national Board as to any matters which require disposition in intervals between meetings of the Board, provided all such matters shall be reported promptly to the Board and, unless moot, shall be subject to ratification by the Board; and provided also that the Board may delegate to or withdraw from the Executive Committee such powers as it may determine.

(E) All persons who are members of the national Board of Directors, the National Advisory Council or the board of an affiliate (or chapter), or a committee or other agency of any of the above, and all persons who are members of any staff, shall be unequivocally committed to the objects of this Union as set forth in Section 2 above, and to the concept of democratic government and civil liberties for all people.

(F) A member of the national Board of Directors or the National Advisory Council may be suspended or removed from his or her position—after hearing, if he or she desires—by vote of a majority of the actual membership of the national Board of Directors.

SECTION 8. *Officers and Committees*

(A) The officers of the Corporation, who shall be members of the Union, shall be a chairperson, a secretary and one or more assistant secretaries, a treasurer and one or more assistant treasurers, one or more general counsel, and an executive director. The officers of the National Advisory Council, who shall be members of the National Advisory Council, shall be a chairperson and two or more vice-chairpersons (distributed among the main geographical sections). The officers of the national Board of Directors, who shall be members of the national Board of Directors, shall be a chairperson, one or more vice-chairpersons, a secretary, and any other which it may from time to time create. The officers of the Corporation, the National Advisory Council and the national Board of Directors shall be elected by the national Board of Directors at the time of or as soon as possible after the annual meeting of the Corporation, for one-year terms. Between annual elections, the national Board of Directors may fill any vacancy among the officers of the Corporation, the National Advisory Council or the national Board of Directors for the remainder of its term; and all officers shall hold office at the pleasure of the national Board. The special nominating committee provided in Section 7 (D) 1) shall be responsible for nominations for all officers of the Corporation, of the National Advisory Council, and of the national Board of Directors, and the election of such officers shall be held at a regular meeting of the national Board.

(B) The Nominating Committee shall be responsible for nominations of persons to be elected to the National Advisory Council and to the national Board of Directors. The Committee shall be composed of five persons, one of them to be designated as chairman, and shall be appointed by the chairman of the corporation, with the advice and consent of the national Board, at the time of or as soon as possible after the annual meeting of the corporation; provided that two members shall be members of affiliate boards (appointed after seeking suggestions from all affiliates), two shall be members of the national Board of Directors, and one shall be a member of the National Advisory Council; and provided also that no more than two members shall be appointed for a second consecutive term and that none shall be appointed for more than two consecutive terms. The terms of the members of the Nominating Committee shall be one year.

(C) The Biennial Conference Committee shall be responsible for overall planning and conduct of each Biennial Conference.

1) It shall act as an arrangements committee in respect to the Conference, receiving from affiliates, the national Board, the National Advisory Council, and other interested parties suggestions and proposals in respect to the program, agenda, and structure of the Conference.

2) It shall establish and propose for adoption by each Biennial Conference an agenda and such rules as it considers necessary or appropriate.

3) It shall be composed of seven persons, and shall be appointed by the chairperson of the Corporation, with the advice and consent of the national Board; provided that no more than three shall be members of the national Board of Directors, and one shall be a member of the National Advisory Council. The remaining three members shall be recommended by the immediately preceding Biennial Conference. Provided, that no member of the Committee shall be appointed for more than two consecutive terms and also provided that no more than three members shall be appointed for a second consecutive term.

4) The terms of the members of the Committee shall expire following the Biennial Conference, on the date upon which their successors are designated.

(D) The national Board of Directors may from time to time create any committee or other agency of the Board which it deems desirable. The chairman and members of each such committee or agency shall be appointed by the chairman of the Board, with the advice and consent of the Board. All such appointees shall hold office at the pleasure of the Board.

SECTION 9. *Corporation and Board Meetings*

(A) The annual meeting of the Corporation shall be held at a time and place to be fixed by the national Board of Directors, and a special meeting may be called by the chairman of the Corporation. Twenty members of the Union shall constitute a quorum.

(B) Regular meetings of the national Board of Directors shall be held at times and places to be fixed by the Board, but the Board shall hold not less than four meetings during each year. Additional meetings shall be convened upon request of the chairman of the Corporation, of five members of the Executive Committee, or of fifteen members of the Board. One third of the actual membership of the Board shall constitute a quorum, except as provided in Sections 10(C) and 12(A) herein. Members of the National Advisory Council and affiliate boards shall be entitled to attend and to participate in discussion but without vote. On request of any three Board members, the Board vote on any motion shall be taken by name and so recorded in the minutes. Absences by any member from three consecutive regular meetings of the Board, without the grant of leave of absence by the Board, shall constitute a resignation from the Board, provided that the Board, in its discretion, may reinstate any member who has resigned in such manner.

(C) By petition, any resolution adopted by the boards of any five affiliates shall be placed upon the agenda of the next following meeting of the national Board of Directors for action.

SECTION 10. *Biennial Conference*

(A) A conference shall be held biennially in odd-numbered years and at a time and place to be fixed by the national Board of Directors, provided that at least each second time it shall be held in a city other than that of the national headquarters (preferably in rotation among the main geographical sections). The first such conference held after January 1, 1978, shall be held in 1979. Affiliate board members, other duly authorized representatives, and professional employees of ACLU or affiliates may attend the conference, and speak at the discretion of the chair. Delegates entitled to vote and to speak shall be as follows: all members of the national Board and National Advisory Council; and further delegates selected by affiliates, the number of which shall be determined according to the following formula:

No. of members in affiliate	Voting delegates
1–499	1
500–1199	2
1200–2199	3
2200–3499	4
3500–6499	5
6500–9999	6
10,000–13,999	7
14,000–up	8

In voting at a Biennial Conference, no delegate shall cast more than one vote; no proxy votes shall be cast or counted; and no affiliate shall have authority to bind or impose any form of unit rule upon its voting delegates. A roll-call vote shall be taken and recorded in the minutes at the request of ten or more delegates.

(B) The Conference may consider any matter of concern to the Union, and may make binding recommendations thereon to the national Board of Directors.

1) The Biennial Conference Committee shall circulate to the affiliates and the national Board of Directors the agenda and the rules it will propose to the Biennial Conference no less than 120 days before the Biennial Conference. Should any affiliate board or any ten members of the national Board propose, no less than 45 days before the Biennial Conference, any addition or amendment to the agenda or the rules as circulated, the Committee shall consider the proposal and either accept or reject it. In either case, the Committee shall promptly notify the affiliates and the delegates to the Biennial Conference of the proposed addition or amendment and of the action the Committee has taken in respect to each such proposal.

2) The Conference shall, at its first meeting, consider the agenda and the rules proposed by the Committee. Adoption of any addition or amendment proposed 45 days or more before the Biennial Conference, if moved by any delegate and seconded, shall be by a simple majority vote of the delegates voting, a quorum being present (a quorum being a majority of registered delegates.)

Adoption of any addition or amendment not previously proposed and not included in the notice to the affiliates and the delegates, if moved by any delegate with ten supporting delegate signatures, shall be by a two-thirds vote of the delegates voting, a quorum being present.

3) The adoption of the agenda and of the rules shall be by a simple majority. Once adopted, the agenda and the rules shall not be amended or suspended except by a two-thirds vote of the delegates voting, a quorum being present.

The Conference may consider any matter of concern to the Union and may make binding recommendations thereon to the national Board of Directors.

(C) The substance of any binding recommendation made by the Conference shall be considered adopted by the national Board of Directors unless the Board shall within 18 months from the time such Conference shall adjourn at a meeting thereof decide otherwise by a majority vote of those present, a quorum being a majority of its actual membership, such vote to be taken by name and so recorded in the minutes.

Such a decision not to adopt a Conference recommendation shall then be submitted for referendum vote. Participants in the referendum shall be members of the board of an affiliate. They shall cast their vote at a meeting of the affiliate or chapter board especially called for the purpose of fully considering the issues in the referendum. Following the meeting the affiliate shall certify to the national office the names of affiliate board members who attended and voted in the referendum. The ballots of members of the affiliate board not present at the meeting shall be returned to the national office. The vote of the affiliate shall be based on the number of members of the affiliate divided by the number of affiliate board members present and voting at the meeting. If the decision of the national Board is over-ridden by a two-thirds vote, then the Board shall adopt the Conference recommendation: provided however, that, as required by the laws of the State of New York governing membership corporations, the national Board of Directors is finally responsible for preventing any action not conforming to the object of the Union as stated in the certificate of incorporation, any act basically threatening the continuation of the Union's business, or any action on matters of administration so detailed as to be entirely within the Board's management.

SECTION 11. *Advice*

(A) Whenever the national office deems any matter to be sufficiently important, it shall immediately seek advice thereon from National Advisory Council members and affiliates, especially by providing them as soon as possible with all working papers supplied to members of the national Board of Directors, or any committee or agency thereof, in connection with meeting agenda items.

(B) In addition, any member of the National Advisory Council or of any affiliate board may on request obtain copies of such working papers, and may take the initiative in raising any question and offering advice thereon.

(C) Immediately on receiving any such question or advice, the national office shall transmit it to the national Board of Directors, or the appropriate committee or other agency thereof, in the same manner as with any question or advice from a national Board member.

SECTION 12. *Amendments*

(A) Amendments to this constitution may be proposed as recommendations of a Biennial Conference. Any amendment so proposed shall be adopted by the national Board of Directors unless the Board shall at a meeting thereof decide otherwise by a majority vote of those present, a quorum being a majority of its actual membership, such vote to be taken by name and so recorded in the minutes. Such a decision not to adopt such a proposed amendment shall then be submitted for referendum vote in accordance with the procedures set forth in Section 7(C) 1) above for the annual election of national Board members and, if the decision of the Board is overridden by a two-thirds vote, the proposed amendment shall thereupon become part of this constitution: provided however that as required by the laws of the State of New York governing membership corporations, the national Board of Directors is finally responsible for preventing any action not conforming to the object of the Union as stated in the certificate of incorporation, any action basically threatening the continuation of the Union's business or any action on matters of administration so detailed as to be entirely within the Board's management.

(B) Amendments may also be proposed by petition of any five members of the national Board of Directors, any ten members of the National Advisory Council, the boards of any three affiliates, or any fifty members of the Union. If such an amendment is approved by the national Board of Directors, it shall then be submitted for referendum vote in accordance with the procedure set forth in Section 7 (C) 1) above for the annual election of national Board members; and if approved by a two-thirds vote, shall thereupon become part of this constitution.

(C) Amendments may also be proposed by petition of the boards of any ten affiliates. Upon receipt of such petition, the national office shall refer the proposed amendment to the national Board for its consideration and subsequently shall submit the proposed amendment together with the Board's recommendation, if any, for referendum vote in accordance with the procedures set forth in Section 7 (C) 1) above for the annual election of national Board members. If approved by a two-thirds vote, the amendment shall become part of the constitution: provided however that as required by the laws of the State of New York governing membership corporations, the national Board of Directors is finally responsible for preventing any action not conforming to the object of the Union as stated in the certificate of incorporation, any action basically threatening the continuation of the Union's business or any action on matters of administration so detailed as to be entirely within the Board's management.

SECTION 13. *Policy Referendum System*

Upon petition of the boards of any ten affiliates, any action taken by the national Board of Directors shall be submitted to a referendum in accordance with the procedures set forth in Section 10(C) of this Constitution.

Board of Directors

Policy #502

Board Elections

It is inappropriate for staff to use the resources of the Union, or in concert with others, to seek to elect or defeat any person duly nominated for any national office.

Staff (national or local) shall have the right to communicate their suggestions in writing or orally to a national nominating committee as a whole, but not to individual members thereof.

If a question arises in the course of an election as to whether or not a violation has taken place, the Executive Committee shall undertake an investigation of the matter, report the facts to the Board, and take such action as it deems appropriate. [Board Minutes, April 19-20, 1969.]

Election Procedures

(a) *Obtaining Affiliate Board Lists; Access to Lists of Electors*
1) Affiliate executive directors shall be notified each April that their up-to-date affiliate Board lists must be received in the national office no later than June 20. Lists or individual changes submitted after that date will not be honored. Ballots will be mailed only to affiliate Board members whose names appear on lists received by June 20.

2) Each nominee shall be informed that he or she may, upon request, receive the lists of the ACLU electorate or any part thereof, for the purpose of communicating with electors regarding the election. Any elector who wishes to communicate with other electors may also upon request receive the lists or parts thereof for the purpose of communicating with electors regarding the election.

3) Any person obtaining the electoral lists or parts thereof for the purpose of communicating with electors, as described in Rule (a)2, shall not in any manner identify the ACLU as the source of the mailing, nor use ACLU letterhead or envelopes.

4) No affiliate, sub-unit of an affiliate, or national chapter may use its funds or personnel for the purpose of supporting or opposing any candidate. This rule prohibits use of the affiliate letterhead or of affiliate funds to pay costs of a mailing supporting or opposing any candidate.[1] [Board Minutes, March 4-5, 1978.]

***

(b) *Mailing of Election Materials*
1) The associate director shall mail all election material no later than the first week in July. [Board Minutes, June 18-19, 1977.]

2) The deadline for receipt of ballots shall be August 31. [Board Minutes, March 4-5, 1978.]

3) Before the election material is mailed, the associate director shall check the National Board and affiliate Board envelopes and remove any duplication.

4) The election materials shall include the ballot, the individual candidate essay, a white plain envelope and a return envelope. There shall be no distinction on the ballot among candidates based upon method of nomination. The ballot shall be placed in the white envelope and then sealed. The sealed envelope shall be placed in the return envelope which on the back shall contain space for the elector's name and ACLU affiliation (affiliate or national Board). The elector shall indicate in which capacity he or she votes. Each elector shall be asked to print his or her name to facilitate counting of votes.

5) At the time the mailing is made, the associate director shall provide the comptroller with a list of those to whom ballots have been mailed.

6) If an affiliate executive director or an affiliate elector reports that an

---

[1] The prohibition of such assistance implements Policy #502 on page 121, which states: "It is inappropriate for staff to use the resources of the Union, or in concert with others, to seek to elect or defeat any person duly nominated for any national office." This policy extends to requests for the electoral lists or parts thereof and to the preparation and dissemination of petitional nominations on behalf of a candidate.

affiliate elector has lost the ballot or did not receive one, the comptroller shall mail another ballot to the individual elector and mark the electoral list accordingly. The same procedure shall apply to a national Board elector. The comptroller shall not respond to any request for information about the balloting, except in connection with an elector's reporting a lost ballot or non-receipt of the ballot.[1]

***

(c) *Receipt and Storing of Ballots Prior to Counting*

The return envelope shall be addressed to the comptroller. No employee of the ACLU shall inspect the envelopes as they are returned. Each day's receipt of envelopes shall be locked by the comptroller in the office safe and remain there until they are prepared for counting.

***

(d) *Preparation of Envelopes for Counting*

1) As soon as the deadline for receipt of ballots has passed, the ballots shall be taken by the comptroller from the safe and grouped into affiliate and national Board sections. The affiliate section shall be organized in alphabetical order. The comptroller shall receive whatever secretarial assistance is needed to organize the ballots. The comptroller shall check each section with the master list to determine if any person has voted twice. If so, the first ballot shall be retained and the second discarded.

2) Any ballot that is unsigned shall be invalid. Any ballot where the signature is illegible shall not be counted. If there is doubt, the comptroller shall consult the executive director, associate director, and membership director (or any two of them) to determine the signature.

As soon as the ballots have been prepared for counting, they shall be made secure again in the comptroller's locked safe until the actual counting begins.

***

(e) *Selection of Tellers*

1) The comptroller shall notify the personnel director when the counting will take place.

2) The personnel director shall obtain through local college-university employment offices a list of people willing to count the votes. On a random sample basis, the personnel director shall employ as many persons as necessary to count the ballots expeditiously.

3) If an emergency arises and a teller does not appear, the personnel director may choose from among the ACLU secretarial staff to fill that teller's place.

***

(f) *Tallying and Retention of Ballots*

1) In addition to the comptroller, a member of the Constitution Committee shall be present throughout the counting of votes. This person shall be appointed

---

[1] The Board approved the recommendation of the Constitution Committee that the office make available what information it can on affiliate or national Board voting in past elections. This would be in response to specific questions on past elections, but not the current election.

by the Chairperson of the Board, and shall determine any question that arises with respect to the interpretation of these rules during the tallying of the ballots.

2) Any candidate may request to know the time at which the tallying will take place, and may designate in writing an observer to be present during the count. Any candidate or designated observer may inspect the tally sheets or the completed statistical chart. (See (g) 2) below.)

3) The tallying of the ballots shall be conducted in the manner prescribed in section (i) of these rules.

4) Once the ballots have been counted, the ballots and returned envelopes shall be brought back to the comptroller's office and secured in the locked safe. They shall be kept there until after the Board meeting at which new Board members are seated.

***

(g) *Statistical Tabulation of Votes*

1) Before the counting of votes begins, the membership director shall have the Membership Department prepare a table of weighted votes for each affiliate and the national Board. The tabulation shall be produced according to Policy 504 in the Policy Guide.

2) The comptroller, with whatever assistance is necessary from the Membership Department, shall be responsible for preparing and executing the final statistical chart of election results.

***

(h) *Certification of Election Results*

1) Once the election results are completed, the comptroller shall certify the results to the executive director.

2) A memorandum shall then be sent to the national Board, affiliates and National Advisory Council, giving the results, including the number of votes received by each candidate.

***

(i) *Detailed Procedures for Counting Ballots*

1) Before the tellers assemble, the comptroller, with whatever secretarial assistance is needed, shall prepare tally sheets for each affiliate and the national Board. The names of the candidates shall appear in the same order as the actual ballot. Each sheet shall be divided into a first count tally column and a second count tally column. Space also shall be left on the upper right hand margin for the initials of the tellers. Each affiliate sheet should be wrapped around the corresponding group of affiliate envelopes. The national Board tally sheet should be wrapped around the national Board envelopes.

2) All tellers shall be given in advance prepared instruction specifying the procedures for counting the ballots, including the following:

1. no information concerning the tally shall be disclosed;
2. selecting at random any of the affiliate groupings;
3. checking each envelope in the grouping to double check whether the correct envelope has been placed in the correct affiliate section;

4. opening the signed envelope and separating it from the inner sealed white envelope containing the ballot; and placing all signed envelopes to one side;

5. opening the white unsigned envelopes and arranging all ballots for counting; the white unsigned envelopes are then discarded;

6. before counting the ballots checking the source on each ballot to determine if it is in the correct affiliate pile;

7. checking the ballot to see if the voter has voted for more candidates than the number specified both on the instruction sheet and the ballot itself. If the voter has voted for more candidates than specified, such ballots are voided. Ballots with fewer votes than the total allowed are counted;

8. counting votes with one teller calling off the name and the other marking it on the tally sheet;

9. after placing the tellers' initials in the box provided wrapping the tally sheet, ballots and signed envelopes with a rubber band and depositing the material in a separate carton;

10. repeating steps 1-8 with each group of envelopes until all affiliate and national Board votes have been counted;

11. for purposes of accurate tallying, when all the ballots have been counted once, a second tally is made by repeating steps 5-9. Where a discrepancy occurs, the two teams of tellers together recount the entire affiliate or national Board vote to discover where the error occurred. When the correct vote is determined, the tally sheets are corrected. [Board Minutes, June 18-19, 1977.]

Policy #503

Election of Executive Committee

Following nominations by the Special Nominating Committee, the Executive Committee is elected by the Board of Directors under a weighted voting-mandatory vote system.

Under this system, the voter lists his or her choices for the Committee in order of preference. The voter designates a preference only for as many candidates as there are places to be filled, but is required to vote for as many candidates as there are available positions. The winners are the candidates receiving the highest numerical vote. The voter designates the preference in numerical order, with the largest numeral first. For example, if there are five vacancies to be filled the voter indicates his or her preferences by placing a 5 beside the name of his or her first choice, a 4 beside the name of the second choice, a 3 beside the name of the third choice, a 2 beside the name of the fourth choice, and a 1 beside the name of the fifth choice. The numbers cast for each candidate are then totaled and the five candidates receiving the highest numerical vote are the winners. [Board Minutes, September 24-25, 1977.]

Funds

Policy #504

Membership—Income Sharing—Primary Membership Responsibility—Development

Uniform Rules for Counting and Maintaining ACLU Membership

Once the national Board has established membership categories, all affiliates are bound to abide by them. The Board may specifically grant one or another affiliate the privilege of establishing different membership categories on an experimental basis. Under such circumstances, an affiliate may suggest higher giving categories to members in its territory, provided that all materials advertising such categories also advise prospects of the basic membership rates adopted by the Board.

At its December 4-5, 1976, meeting, the Board adopted these membership categories:

	Individual	*Joint*
Life Member	$1000	$1000
Sponsoring Member	125	125
Sustaining Member	75	75
Contributing Member	35	50
Basic Membership	20	30
Limited Income Membership	5	—

Members of the ACLU shall be considered members both of the national organization and of the affiliate in which they reside or to which they contribute. All affiliates will promptly notify the national office of the change in any member's address.

Members moving from one affiliate to another automatically have their membership transferred to the new affiliate and relinquished by the old one, except at the expressed written request of the member.

All persons contributing the minimum amounts provided by the national Board are accepted as members, with those accounts indicating dual membership being counted as two persons for membership counts.

For weighting of votes of national and affiliate Board members in elections of national Board of Directors and referenda, a member is counted if he or she has contributed for the present year or for the preceding year. (A referendum taken in September 1972 would be based on a membership count of those who have given for 1972 or 1971. This would include some new members whose last contribution may have been as early as October 1970.)

Each affiliate obligates itself to maintain such practices and procedures on these matters as may be determined from time to time by the ACLU Board.

The Board shall establish uniform requirements for reporting verification of the procedures followed by PMR affiliates to assure uniform practices throughout the Union—and shall direct the Director of Membership to audit reports filed by the affiliates pursuant to those requirements:

1) Prior to each election of members of the national Board of Directors, and/or national referendum, the Director shall cause to be run off on the national computer a count of members of all national PMR affiliates, and all PMR affiliates sharing the national computer, on the following basis:

a) all members having contributed for the current and/or past year shall be counted.

b) no individual shall be counted as a member whose last recorded annual contribution shall be less than the minimum membership prescribed by the Board of Directors (in 1972—$5).

c) all individual members shall be counted as one; and all dual members shall be counted as two, irrespective of the amount of their contribution, subject to (b) above.

2) Affiliates not sharing the national computer shall complete and return the questionnaire to the national office with membership counts as of April 1 and October 1 of each year, or such date as may be closest to any election to the national Board of Directors or referendum. The count of each affiliate's members thus submitted shall be used in weighting the votes of national and affiliate board members in the election or referendum next following receipt of the questionnaire.

Should an affiliate fail to fill out and return the questionnaire prior to the counting of ballots for any national Board election or referendum as specified above, the previous verified count submitted on this questionnaire shall be used for the purpose of weighting the votes of national Board members, and the vote of its affiliate Board members, provided that should the affiliate have failed to submit a verified count of members within twelve months preceding any election or referendum, the votes of its affiliate board members shall be counted as one each. [Board Minutes, December 5-7, 1969, amended February 14-15, 1970.]

National-Affiliate Income Sharing

Membership Income: Under the standard sharing formula, the ACLU entity, national office or affiliate, which recruits a new member, shall retain in full the first year's proceeds of that membership. When a member renews for the year, a $2.50 PMR (primary membership responsibility) charge is deducted from the renewal. The affiliate to which the member belongs then receives 52% of the rest of the renewal, or any subsequent contribution the member may make to the organization within the contribution year, with 45 1/2% going to the national organization, and 2 1/2% to the Crisis Area Fund. [Board Minutes, December 3-4, 1977.]

The PMR factor of $2.50 goes to the entity (national or affiliate) which performs the PMR function. [Board Minutes, November 19, 1962, September 28, 1964.]

The following provisions must accompany the formula:

1) $2.50 per member will be rebated from National to PMR affiliates. (The $2.50 PMR fee, presently taken off the top of each renewal, is now built into the 45 1/2% National share.)

2) Affiliates will not be taxed additionally for the Biennial Conference. The Biennial will now be financed completely out of the National budget. A separate account is to be set up in the National budget for Biennial costs. This allocation should be made on an annual basis so that the money is available in the year in which the Biennial Conference is held.

3) The formula is to be reviewed in two years, in order to evaluate its effect and to assess its equity in light of changes that may take place in average membership contribution. [Board Minutes, December 3-4, 1977.]

Definition of a NEW member for sharing purposes: A former member of ACLU can be counted as "new" for sharing purposes when no contribution has been received from him or her for the two calendar years preceding the one in which he or she rejoined the Union. (e.g.: A member rejoins ACLU in 1969; the last previous contribution was in 1967; this is a renewal; the last contribution was in 1966; this is new.) [Staff Memo, 1966.]

New members joining after October 1 of each year will have their contributions credited to the following year (to avoid immediate billing under the "All-At-Once" renewal system).

Special Geographical Considerations

In recognition of the problems raised by the unique geographic character of the District of Columbia and the National Capital Area CLU, the following sharing formula will apply to membership income from the Montgomery County and Prince George's County chapters of the ACLU of Maryland: National ACLU 20%; National Capital Area CLU 30%; ACLU of Maryland 50%. Members residing in the suburban chapters shall continue to hold dual membership in the National Capital Area CLU and the state affiliate, the ACLU of Maryland.

In the case of the Northern Virginia chapter, the following formula, if chosen by both the Virginia affiliate and the Northern Virginia chapter, shall apply: (1) effective December 1, 1973 the Northern Virginia chapter shall no longer have dual affiliation and shall be within the sole and exclusive jurisdiction of the ACLU of Virginia: (2) present members of the Northern Virginia chapter may choose to remain members of either the National Capital Area CLU or the ACLU of Virginia under procedures established by the national office with approval of the Executive Committee; new and transferred members of the Northern Virginia chapter, who have substantial contact with the national capital area, may choose to become members of either the National Capital Area

CLU or the ACLU of Virginia under procedures to be established by the national office with approval of the Executive Committee;[1] (3) membership income will be shared with national ACLU on the basis of the regular 60-40% formula;[2] (4) if the arrangement has a substantial adverse impact upon the National Capital Area CLU's 1974 income, the national Board may consider ameliorative measures. [Board Minutes, September 29-30, 1973.]

Unshared Income

The raising of unshared income by affiliates is permitted under the following conditions:

1) Each project must be conceived and carried out so as not to interfere with the *advance of* joint membership income from the affiliate's area.

2) As a normal rule, all such projects should involve the provisions of something of money's worth for the money paid, such as a theater benefit or a garden party.

(Rule 2 has been interpreted to mean that an affiliate may retain the whole proceeds of a theater benefit, banquet, reception (with fixed admission charge), etc. Should such an event be the occasion for soliciting pledges or donations to the work of the organization, however, the proceeds from such a campaign must be shared with the national organization.)

3) As a general rule, whenever contributions are solicited, the proceeds should become joint membership income. Moreover, even unsolicited contributions should be presumed to be intended for joint membership income unless an unsolicited direction from the donor clearly designates the affiliate or the national treasury to retain it. *The mere naming of the national organization or one affiliate in the remittance will not be regarded as such a designation.* However, unsolicited contributions specifically designating an affiliate may be retained by the affiliate.

4) In special, non-recurring circumstances unshared contributions may be solicited for a "cause" such as an unusually expensive case in litigation or to enable an unstaffed affiliate to become staffed. For any major "cause" solicitation, however, a written proposal should first be made for the approval of the Steering Committee of the National Development Council (which may be obtained by written poll of its members unless they determine a meeting to be

[1] This arrangement was amended by the Executive Committee on September 27, 1974 and reported to the Board of Directors on December 7, 1974 without objection. The new provision provides that "Any new member of the ACLU residing in Virginia or any member who transfers residency to Virginia shall be a member of the Virginia affiliate. However, if a new or transfer member is employed in the District of Columbia area and requests to be a member of the D.C. affiliate and uses a D.C. area address then that member shall be a member of the D.C. affiliate."

[2] Although the Board adopted a new sharing formula at the December 1977 Board meeting, the present formula will continue in effect for Montgomery, Prince George's counties, which have a special arrangement for sharing between National, Maryland and the National Capital area.

necessary), detailing the need for and intended employment of the funds to be solicited, and the precautions being employed to avoid interference with the advance of joint membership income.

5) All local, unshared fund-raising projects should be designed to employ a minimum of staff time and preferably to enlist the talent of volunteers who would not otherwise find an ACLU outlet for their talents.

6) Special precautions should be taken to avoid timing any such local projects during the period of ordinary membership renewals (for affiliates on a calendar-year renewal basis) or at the time of the usual national special funds appeal (for affiliates in areas to which these are addressed).

7) All local, unshared fund-raising projects should be fully reported to the Steering Committee, through the national membership director, in sufficient detail so that successes and failures can be analyzed and reported for the benefit of other affiliates. All individual contributions, retained under the provisions of 3 and 4, above, in amounts of $25 or more should likewise be reported, with name and address of contributor and amount and date of contribution, for inclusion on the member's record.

(Rule 7 has fallen into disuse, except to the extent that affiliates have reported for tax or audit purposes.) [Board Minutes, May 15, 1963.]

(See policy on American Civil Liberties Union Foundation, Inc. for rules governing sharing of tax-deductible income.)

Bequest Income

Bequests received by an affiliate or by the national organization are not shared, unless a sharing agreement is in force between that affiliate and the national organization. The following is the text of the sharing agreement which has been approved by the Board:

1) The sharing formula hereinafter defined shall apply to all unrestricted legacies either to the American Civil Liberties Union, Inc., this affiliate or any of its chapters in the will of a decedent who was a member of the affiliate or a domiciliary of the affiliate territory, who dies during the term of this agreement regardless of when distribution may be made, and in the will of any such person. who dies during the term of any previous sharing agreement to the extent that such legacy has not been distributed, notwithstanding any provision in such sharing agreement to the contrary, provided, however, that it shall not apply where the testator has specifically excluded either the national organization or the affiliate or specifically provided for some other method of sharing. Disputes over the appropriate affiliate to share shall be resolved by the national Board of the American Civil Liberties Union, Inc., or a committee or outside arbitrator designated thereby.

a) Each and every individual bequest made to the American Civil Liberties Union, Inc. shall be shared with the affiliate initially receiving whichever of the following two amounts is smaller and the remainder payable to the Vigilance Fund of the American Civil Liberties Union, Inc.:

(i) An amount equal to 100% of the operating expenses of the affiliate in the year preceding the death of the testator.

(ii) 40% of the bequest.

In those cases where (i) is smaller, the affiliate may request within a year from the Steering Committee, or another committee as may be designated by the national Board, an amount up to but not exceeding the difference between (i) and (ii) to implement a program which shall be described in a proposal submitted to the Steering Committee. The Steering Committee may allocate an amount of up to the difference after consultation with the affiliate leadership on the proposed program. Rejection by the Steering Committee of an affiliate proposal is subject to review by the national Board which shall exercise final jurisdiction.

b) Each individual bequest made to the affiliates shall be shared with the affiliate initially receiving whichever of the following two amounts is smaller and the remainder payable to the Vigilance Fund of the American Civil Liberties Union, Inc.:

(i) An amount equal to 100% of the operating expenses of the affiliate in the year preceding the death of the testator.

(ii) An amount equal to 60% of the bequest.

In those cases where (i) is smaller, the affiliate may receive the difference between (i) and (ii) by following the procedure outlined above.

(iii) "Operating expenses" in the above formula shall be based on a certified public audit on an accrual accounting basis excluding the national share of membership income and all bookkeeping reserves. "Operating expenses" under both a) (i) and b) (i) of this contract shall include the combined expenses of both taxed and untaxed affiliate activities.

(iv) This agreement shall continue until the end of the third full calendar year next succeeding the date hereof. This agreement shall be automatically renewed from year to year unless terminated by notice given before December 1st in any year after a resolution to that effect adopted by the board of the affiliate, or by the Board of Directors of the American Civil Liberties Union, Inc. Such termination shall then occur as of midnight of December 31 of the same year but such termination shall have no effect on legacies under wills of persons who have previously died or die prior to January 1st of the following year and payments under such wills shall be shared as provided in this agreement regardless of when made.

(v) Neither party may enter into a new sharing agreement until the expiration of a full year after the termination of an earlier agreement, and such new agreement shall have no application to any legacy under a will of a person dying between the date of the termination of this agreement and the execution of any new agreement.

(vi) Parties to this contract agree that they will not solicit legacies which are not subject to the terms of this agreement. [Board Minutes, Sept. 26-27, June, 1971.]

Affiliate Indebtedness

A floating interest rate, subject to quarterly adjustment of one percent in excess of the prime rate or half percent in excess of the actual rate currently being paid by the national office, whichever is greater, shall apply to indebtedness of affiliates to the national office. With respect to existing debts, no affiliate shall be charged a rate of interest in excess of this formula or in excess of any lower rate that had been negotiated previously. [Board Minutes, March 5-6, 1977.]

Primary Membership Responsibility (PMR)

Definition: Primary membership responsibility (PMR) is defined as the function of maintaining complete membership records, soliciting members for renewals and increased contributions, and maintaining pledge billing programs. Either the national office or any affiliate may perform the PMR function. PMR affiliates do their own collecting of funds and remit a monthly statement to the national office, along with a check for national's share of such contributions, calculated according to the standard sharing formula. Members in areas for which the national organization has PMR send their membership contributions to the national office.

Conditions for Assumption of PMR: An affiliate wishing to take over the PMR function from the national office must send a request to the Steering Committee of the National Development Council early in the year preceding the one for which it wishes to assume PMR. Such a request must be accompanied by a showing that the affiliate is prepared to handle the mechanical aspects of PMR and to use the opportunity PMR affords to improve shared membership income. PMR affiliates undertake not to solicit membership income from members who have moved out of their geographic area. Petitions for PMR should be accompanied by a financial report for the previous year, a budget for the year in which the petition is made, projections of income and expenses for three years ahead, and a description of the affiliate's program. It should preferably be supported by a team of lay and staff leaders of the affiliate, meeting with the Steering Committee in person. [Board Minutes, April 15, 1963; Minutes of Joint Finance Committee, March 2, 1963.]

All new PMR affiliates shall receive PMR on a two-year trial basis with a review procedure to be implemented before extension is approved. [Board Minutes, September 29-30, 1973.]

Remittance of the National Share of Income: PMR affiliates are required to remit to the national office 1/3 of all membership income collected each month not later than the tenth day of the following month. Adjustment to the exact national-affiliate share will be made upon submission of the affiliate PMR report. [Board Minutes, Sept. 27, 1970.]

Centralized Data Processing: Upon assurance of improved computer operations, all PMR affiliates will transfer their record keeping to the national computer, in a manner calculated to achieve a gradual adjustment in affiliate mailing schedules. The Board will fix per-member charges for computer services which will fairly allocate between national and affiliates the economies affectuated by consolidated record-keeping. [Board Minutes, Sept. 27, 1970.]

Conditions for the Retention of PMR: 1) *Annual Review.* The Steering Committee will adopt procedures for annual review of the development performance of all affiliates receiving the PMR subsidy, and where appropriate, will recommend to the national Board removal of PMR status. [Board Minutes, Sept. 27, 1970.]

2) *Interest on Delinquency.* Any affiliate which fails to remit the national share of membership income by the end of the month following the month of collection, or which fails to repay scheduled loans, shall be charged interest at the rate of 10 percent per annum with any portion of the month to be counted as a whole month. [Board Minutes, December 14, 1968; October 5, 1969; September 27, 1970; June 12, 1974.]

3) *Guaranteed Income Sharing* (GIS). Should a PMR affiliate fall two months in arrears in remitting the national share of membership income, the national staff will notify the affiliate that it must institute GIS with respect to all membership contributions received. Such contributions will be deposited in full in a bank account opened by the national office in the affiliate's headquarters city. Deposit slips will be mailed to the national office, which in turn will promptly send the affiliate a check for 2/3 of each deposit, less 1/12 of the accrued affiliate PMR indebtedness monthly, until the affiliate debt is liquidated. Should affiliate delinquency result in a second institution of GIS within a twelve month period, the GIS procedure will remain in effect for a full twelve months, regardless of repayment. [Board Minutes, December 5, 1970, entered as correction of omission of motion adopted September 27, 1970.]

4) *Removal of PMR Status.* After a PMR affiliate has become sixty days delinquent on any indebtedness to the national organization, the staff will initiate proceedings for taking back PMR, setting forth in detail a proposed effective date and steps for implementation. The staff will present evidence of how well the affiliate has used PMR to increase shared membership income, comparing its increase to the national increase and to that of other affiliates for which national retains PMR. The case will be presented to the affiliate and to the Steering Committee, and the Steering Committee will promptly forward its recommendation on the matter to the Board of Directors, with the ultimate decision whether to withdraw PMR being made by the national Board. [Board Minutes, October 4-5, 1969.]

5) *Return of PMR.* While no change in PMR arrangements will be required at this time, the national office should attempt to persuade affiliates to return PMR. [Board Minutes, September 29-30, 1973.]

Membership Recruitment
The national office should give leadership in terms of techniques, literature and other resources in membership recruitment.

Development and Assistance to Affiliates
The ACLU should work toward having at least one staffed affiliate in every state in the union. [Board Minutes, March 5-6, 1977.]

Policy #509

Crisis Area Fund
The Crisis Area Fund was established to subsidize programs in critical areas where the Union's more accustomed "seed money" support from national funds cannot be expected to produce self-sustaining operations. In its early days, the Crisis Area Fund supported the staffing of the Southern Regional Office and the beleaguered Louisiana affiliate. In recent years the Crisis Area Fund has helped to establish the Mountain States Regional Office, aided affiliates fighting a referendum preserving housing discrimination and assisted numerous affiliates to maintain and improve their program.

In the past, the Fund has been financed from a combination of two sources: affiliates have voluntarily contributed amounts equal to 5%, or more, of their yearly share of regular membership income and the national Board of Directors contributes yearly 10% of the previous year's additions to the Vigilance Fund. [Board Minutes, September 27, 1965, and September 26-27, 1970.]

The Fund is presently financed by the national Board of Director's contribution yearly of 10% of the previous year's additions to the Vigilance Fund and by affiliate contribution of 5% of the affiliate share of "shared and affiliate new income." Crisis Area Fund contributions are mandatory upon every affiliate. Crisis Area Fund money is used solely for purposes of stimulating and assisting affiliate development programs. [Board Minutes, September 30, 1972, National Development Council Steering Committee Minutes, June 4-5, 1971.]

Grants from the Crisis Area Fund are within the sole discretion of the Steering Committee of the National Development Council. All minutes of the Steering Committee regarding Crisis Area Fund appropriations shall be made available to the national Board, and shall be reviewed routinely at the start of every national Board meeting. [Board Minutes, December 9-10, 1972.]

For the year 1974, the affiliate contribution to the Crisis Area Fund is reduced to 4% of the affiliate share of "shared and affiliate new income." [Board Minutes, December 8-9, 1973.]

The 4% assessment of affiliate income for the Crisis Area Fund shall be maintained until further action of the Board. [Board Minutes, December 6-7, 1975.]

The 4% contribution from affiliates for the Crisis Area Fund should be continued in 1977. [Board Minutes, December 4-5, 1976.]

Policy #512

Development/Steering Committee

The Steering Committee of the National Development Council endorses the proposal of the chairperson to add three persons (two National Board members and one member of the National Advisory Council) to the Steering Committee which will then be reconstituted as the Development/Steering Committee of the National Board and of the NDC with the following conditions:

1) The Development/Steering Committee shall conduct an immediate analysis of the proper structure and function of the ACLU Development/Steering Committee and shall report its proposals to the first National Board meeting in 1978;

2) Until that time, the Development/Steering Committee will retain all of the functions of the Steering Committee as defined in Board policies 504, 506, 509, 511;

3) Until that time, the Development/Steering Committee will retain the present membership and structure as defined by Board policy 511, augmented by the three new members;

Until that time, the Development/Steering Committee shall serve both as the Steering Committee of the NDC and as the committee on development of the National Board. The Committee would identify, study and recommend to the Board means to raise income and recruit members which will advance the Union's program on a national basis. [Board Minutes, March 5-6, 1977.]

Litigation

Policy #513

Relations with Counsel

(a) Legal assignments by the ACLU are in no way based on considerations of race or religion. [Board Minutes, March 28, 1960.]

***

(b) Under no circumstances may any cooperating attorney associated in any way with an ACLU or affiliate case receive payment for services rendered in such a case, whether as a fee or voluntary donation. The smallest exception to this rule would jeopardize the voluntary nature of the cooperating system and the effectiveness of ACLU's entire legal program. [Board Minutes, February 14-15, 1970.]

Attorneys' fees granted by a court order shall be retained by ACLU affiliates. [Board Minutes, February 14-15, 1976.]

For a period of two years, the extent to which volunteer cooperating attorneys may share fees awarded by courts will be determined by rules adopted by each affiliate. In the implementation of this experiment, each affiliate intending to share fees with cooperating attorneys shall adopt written procedures in advance of any sharing and the procedures adopted shall be reported to the general counsel of the national organization as shall be the experience of the affiliate under any such procedures. [Board Minutes, March 4-5, 1977.]

An attorney retained full-time on salary by the ACLU or an affiliate should not act as a private counsel in cases involving civil liberties issues except with the consent of the Board or Executive Committee to which he is responsible. Any civil liberties case offered privately to an attorney who is retained on salary by the ACLU or an affiliate, either full-time or part-time, shall be offered first to the Union or to the affiliate for its decision whether to adopt a case as an official ACLU case. These precautions will avoid troublesome conflict of interest problems between employer and employee.

Any lawyer who sits on an official ACLU or affiliate body who is representing a party in a case which comes before the Union or an affiliate, should disclose such an interest in the case immediately. Though thereafter participation in discussion is allowed, the attorney should refrain from voting. [Board Minutes, February 14-15, 1970.]

***

(c) Participation of federal government lawyers in the ACLU's work would seem to fall within the ordinary right of a citizen to participate in public discussion and in such non-partisan political activities as do not create a clear conflict of interest with their obligations to the government. Generally speaking, a governmental lawyer ought to be allowed by the Department of Justice to assist the ACLU provided the ACLU issue does not concern the attorney's own agency or any relevant secret or confidential information of which the attorney has knowledge or access. The lawyer should not be so identified as to appear to "act for" an interested governmental party in a representative capacity. However, the appropriateness or lawfulness of a particular activity should be judged against a context wider than simple conflict of interest, including professional or business relationships, as well as tact and good judgment. [News Release, April 8, 1965; National Capital Area Civil Liberties Union Memo; Staff letter, November 4, 1964.]

POLICY UNDER REVIEW.

Policy #514

Definition of Legal Role

(a) The goal of litigation by the ACLU and its affiliates, in general terms, is to advance understanding and acceptance of civil liberties principles. This goal can be achieved through litigation in one or more of three ways: by persuading the courts and other tribunals to recognize new legal principles; by persuading them to apply established principles, in the frequent instances where they are not fully observed in practice; and by educating the public through the publicity generated by such litigation to an appreciation of the civil liberties principles involved.

Because the resources of the Union are limited, some selectivity must be exercised in deciding which cases should be taken. The ACLU cannot take every case where there is a civil liberties question being raised. Rather, it should direct its efforts to cases which have some reasonable promise of having broad impact on other cases. Thus, it is always appropriate to take a case which offers the possibility of establishing new civil liberties precedents which will control other cases. Where the legal precedent is clear, but is widely ignored in practice, it will be worthwhile for the ACLU to take some cases for the purpose of making the precedent effective.

Although the publicity attending the ACLU's legal activities will have real value in educating the public to a better understanding of the civil liberties principles for which the organization stands, this value will not be achieved, and indeed may be defeated, if the civil liberties issues are obscured or the nature of the organization's interest in a case is misunderstood. This risk, of course, cannot always be entirely avoided, but it is nonetheless a consideration to be kept in mind in deciding the manner in which the organization should participate in a case.

Although the Union formerly did most of its legal work in an *amicus curiae* capacity, in recent years direct representation has come to play an increasingly important role for both the national organization and the affiliates. There are often substantial advantages to be gained by direct representation. They include the opportunity to establish and preserve an appropriate record related to the civil liberties issue which is of interest; the possibility of raising new or additional civil liberties issues which would not otherwise necessarily be involved in a case; and, in some cases, the possibility of securing affirmative relief with a broad effect. An additional consideration sometimes is that a civil liberties claimant would be unable to secure effective legal assistance if the Union did not provide it. The impact on the public is also likely to be greater where there is direct representation, at least in affirmative suits, than where there is only *amicus* participation.

It is not necessary to await clients seeking out the Union; it is often better for the Union to take the initiative in civil liberties cases. *NAACP v. Button* (1963) provides that organizations need not stand by while potential litigants forfeit through ignorance their constitutional rights. The ACLU can thus advise people that it will handle cases for them.

There are some potential organizational problems in direct representation. Almost invariably it will require more effort and expense than *amicus* participation. There will sometimes be many issues, both factual and legal, which have no civil liberties content but which must nonetheless be dealt with in the course of litigation. Such issues may prevent the civil liberties issue from being reached, either because the civil liberties point rests on an assumed set of facts which does not prove out at trial or because the non-civil liberties issues are dispositive of the proceeding; they may require an inordinate expenditure of time and effort, in relation to the civil liberties issue; and they may obscure the civil liberties issue in the public's understanding of the case. These disadvantages of direct representation will not be of equal importance in every case, and they may be outweighed in a particular instance by other considerations like those discussed in paragraph d. Moreover, there are different kinds of direct representation which will present such disadvantages in differing degrees: representation of a party in a civil suit is quite different from representation of a defendant in a criminal case; and representation on an appeal presents fewer problems than at trial.

The foregoing considerations suggest the following guidelines for deciding whether the Union or an affiliate should participate in a particular case.

1) The case should present a civil liberties issue on which the appropriate Board, national or affiliate, has taken a position. If it does not fall within a general position already so taken, the case should be presented to the Board (or in emergency cases, to an executive committee or other group, such as general counsel, to which such authority has been delegated) for approval. Where more than one civil liberties question is likely to be involved, the position to be taken as to each of them should be so determined.

2) The case should involve a determination of the civil liberties issue in such fashion as to have an impact on other cases beyond the particular one in question, either by establishing a new legal precedent, or by tending to increase significantly the recognition of existing precedent in practice. Particular attention should be paid to this point where direct representation of a defendant is contemplated, since it may be difficult or impossible for the organization's attorney to withdraw if it turns out that the civil liberties issue is not in fact involved.

3) Consideration should, of course, always be given to the possible adverse effects should a case be lost. This consideration is of particular importance where the issue is a novel one and an adverse determination may have a precedential impact. It is always important to select a case which presents the best possible record for a favorable determination of the issue.

4) In the direct representation of plaintiffs in affirmative suits, it is generally possible to specify the issues that will be raised in advance, and as a condition of the organization undertaking to provide legal representation. The issues can often be defined and limited from the start; the case can be so shaped as to point up the civil liberties issues and avoid extraneous ones in a way not ordinarily available in defensive cases; and it is often possible to secure affirmative relief which will be of broad effect.

5) In cases where direct representation will involve the defense of a lawsuit, greater difficulties and hazards are presented, for such cases will sometimes

involve legal and factual issues which have no civil liberties content, and which may overshadow the civil liberties issue. In some cases the party involved may wish to raise only the civil liberties issues in the case. In that case, if it is made perfectly clear to the party what his or her rights are, and he or she chooses without pressure from the organization, direct or otherwise, to forego certain legal points in order to test others, it may be proper to undertake defensive representation on a narrow basis. Where the grounds for the Union's participation are not so limited, its attorney would be remiss in not pressing every issue that may be of use to the party he or she is representing; and the effect of this may be to nullify or diminish the interest of the case from a civil liberties point of view. The uncertainties of direct representation of a defendant at the trial level are often substantially reduced when a case is on appeal, since the legal issues then have been defined and the factual ones largely resolved. The mere fact, however, that the immediate case may be lost is not sufficient to refuse to take it.

6) *Amicus curiae* participation will ordinarily present no problems beyond the simple questions whether an appropriate civil liberties question is involved and whether an *amicus* brief will be helpful to the court and generally advance the purposes of the ACLU. In deciding whether to intervene, the affiliate must judge its own priorities and resources, but a primary consideration should be whether the proposed brief can contribute anything to the case or whether it will simply repeat arguments already made by the litigant's attorney.

In any case where the ACLU or an affiliate has undertaken to furnish a direct representation, the judgment of the attorneys who provide such representation must be governed by the client's interest, not the organization's, since they are acting as attorneys for the client, and not for the ACLU. Where *amicus* participation is involved, the attorneys preparing a brief should be given the usual latitude for the exercise of their professional skills and judgments in the presentation of the issue which the organization has approved, but the organization, or an appropriate delegate, should exercise a right of final approval before a brief is filed.

There should be a clearly understood mechanism for deciding and recording decisions to enter litigation. [Board Minutes, February 14-15, 1970.]

***

(b) The ACLU and its affiliates should not normally undertake to pledge bail. Beyond the question of tying up badly needed funds and the danger of the loss of funds, our lawyers should urge recognizance release whenever this is possible, instead of bail. On rare occasions, bail may be appropriately provided in order to preserve some other constitutional right, especially in an emergency or where there are no other bail sources. The matter must rest with the judgment of the affiliate. [Board Minutes, February 14-15, 1970.]

***

(c) The ACLU and its affiliates encourage, and if necessary will participate in, the formation of general legal services programs for the poor. This does not necessarily imply that the organization will itself provide broad legal services to the poor. However, the Union has encouraged its affiliates to establish staffed offices in the ghettos of large cities as a means of providing effective civil liberties legal services to the poor. [Board Minutes, June 22, 1966, December 2-3, 1967.] (See also policy on Counsel for Indigent, Minorities, Underprivileged Individuals.)

***

(d) A request by an affiliate to have the national office enter a case in the affiliate's geographical area is made by the legal director, and the decision as to whether or not to enter the case is his/her's to make.

Where there is a conflict between an affiliate and the ACLU, ACLU will enter a case in the affiliate area only by a majority vote of the general counsel.

Decisions involved in the above two mentioned paragraphs are appealable to the ACLU Executive Committee and the ACLU Board of Directors. [Board Minutes, February 14-15, 1976.]

Policy #525

National-Affiliate Relations

(a) National chapters may be established as an interim organizational measure in areas where there are insufficient numbers of members to warrant the chartering of an affiliate. Such interim groups may conduct local litigation and education, and hopefully will increase the membership base to the point where an affiliate can be established.

The following rules govern the formation of national chapters:

1) National chapters may be chartered by the national Board or its Executive Committee to function under previously approved by-laws upon the petition of twenty-five or more ACLU members living within the area who indicate a willingness to be active in a local organization and request the establishment thereof, along with the names and brief biographical sketches of the members elected to serve on the initial Executive Committee.

2) A national chapter may be dissolved by the national Board or its Executive Committee at any time at their sole discretion and according to such provisions as they prescribe, provided that no less than thirty days' written notice is sent to every member of that chapter. A national chapter shall be automatically dissolved upon the chartering of an affiliate in the state. [Board Minutes, February 15-16, 1969.]

***

(b) Conflict between the national Board and the affiliates, often being damaging to the larger purposes of the Union, is to be avoided where possible.

To this end, consultation should be initiated, by either party, at the earliest stages in the development of such potential conflict. When an affiliate has adopted or appears likely to adopt a position on an issue which the national Board has not yet considered or on which the national Board has taken a contradictory position, the affiliate should promptly advise the national office of such action or such proposed action, so as to permit national consideration of the issue.

When an affiliate takes a position that conflicts with the national position, it should take great care to announce publicly that its stand is its own.

The national Board or, if time does not allow, the Executive Committee of the national Board may, in its discretion, state publicly that the affiliate's action is its own and does not represent national policy. Such a statement should note the Union policy on affiliate freedom of action within its proper authority.

The affiliate is free to implement its policies as it sees fit. However, in situations where such implementation can impair the Union's credibility and integrity, or the effectiveness of the national program, after a hearing of the affiliate if the affiliate so desires, the national Board, by a two-thirds vote of at least two-thirds of the total membership, may direct an affiliate:

1) To desist from a course of conduct seriously inconsistent with the policies and integrity of the ACLU; and

2) To refrain from a specific action (such as an appearance before a court or legislature) that the Board decides impedes a vital policy or program of the ACLU.

The above guideline is based on the need to protect the purpose of section 6(A) of the ACLU Constitution, in recognition of the specific power given the national Board under section 6(C) of the ACLU Constitution, stating that "an affiliate may be suspended or removed from the Union—after hearing, if the affiliate so desires—by a vote of two-thirds of the actual membership of the national Board of Directors."

An affiliate should refrain from taking action with respect to any matters outside its geographical area without consultation with the affiliate in whose jurisdiction the matter arises and, if practicable, with the national office. In addition some matters arising within a single affiliate's geographic area are distinctly national in character and should be spoken to or acted upon by the affiliate only: (1) to implement national policy, or, (2) in the absence of national policy, only after consultation with the national office. (Matters arising in litigation should be governed by the standards established in the "Guide to ACLU Litigation.") Matters national in character include:

1) The validity of a federal statute, Constitutional amendment, or treaty, or of an interpretation of a federal statute, Constitutional amendment, or treaty;

2) The ACLU position on a proposed federal statute, Constitutional amendment, or treaty, implemented by testimony before a Congressional committee;

3) Activity of a federal officer or of an agency of the federal government having general application as distinct from its field offices;

4) Cases of the kind described in the section "Shared Responsibility for Special Kinds of Cases" from the "Guide to ACLU Litigation";

5) Public comments by one affiliate on events occurring exclusively in the jurisdiction of another;

6) Public comments by an affiliate which concern events that are national in scope.

The national office may enter an individual affiliate area with respect to matters that are not national in scope only after full consultation with the affiliate and only after the affiliate has failed to act to implement national policy.

Each affiliate is responsible for ensuring that the sub-units of the affiliate (chapter or branches), having some independent policy-making authority, operate within the framework of these guidelines. [Board Minutes, December 9-10, 1972.]

A request by an affiliate to have ACLU staff lobby before an affiliate's state legislature shall be reviewed by the ACLU executive director. The decision as to whether or not to have a national staff person lobby before the affiliate's state legislature is his/her's to make.

Where there is disagreement between an affiliate and the ACLU or where an affiliate has not so invited ACLU to lobby before its state legislature, ACLU staff will so lobby only upon the approval of the ACLU executive director or the ACLU chairperson, after consultation with the affiliate. [Board Minutes, February 14-15, 1976.]

ACLU paid staff shall not in their position as paid staff publicly lobby, take cases, or in other ways involve ACLU in issues which have not had prior approval of the ACLU Board of Directors. [Board Minutes, October 2-3, 1976.]

(See also Constitution, policy on Supreme Court cases, and discussion of national-affiliate relations in Introduction.)

Policy #528

Internal Employment

(a) *Affirmative Action*

1) *Introduction:* The American Civil Liberties Union is an equal opportunity employer. In order to ensure equal opportunity and the employment of minorities and women within the ACLU, the ACLU hereby adopts the terms and conditions set forth in this Affirmative Action Plan.

2) *Scope:* This Plan applies to all employees of the ACLU.

3) *Past Practices:* An internal employment audit of each level of employment within the ACLU during the past 10 years shows that the ACLU has

employed very few minorities and women in top level executive positions. Very few minorities and women have been equally employed by the ACLU, and they have been overrepresented in clerical positions.

A review of the ACLU employment practices reveals that recruitment for all positions within the ACLU in the past 10 years has relied primarily upon word-of-mouth recruitment within the ACLU national-affiliate family and upon advertisement within publications which are directed primarily at a white constituency and to a lesser degree at a white male constituency. It is the purpose of this Affirmative Action Plan to provide equal opportunity and to remedy those past practices.

4) *Affirmative Action Officer:* The executive director shall appoint an affirmative action officer who shall be confirmed by the Executive Committee. The officer is responsible for implementation of and monitoring compliance with the Plan, and shall be authorized to spend a reasonable and appropriate amount of time at this task.

5) *Statistics, Reporting, and Annual Review:* The ACLU shall prepare and maintain a table of employees covered by this Plan according to the following categories:

a) Black Men/Women
b) Hispanics Men/Women
c) Oriental and Native American Men/Women
d) Total Women
e) Total Men
f) Grand Total

The listing, covering all ACLU job qualifications, should note persons in jobs paying: 1) $25,000 and up; 2) $17,000-$24,999; and 3) below $17,000.

Inclusion in these categories should be by voluntary choice or by visual identification. An updated copy of this table will be included in the package of materials prepared for the Board of Directors at every Board meeting. A report to be submitted to the Board of Directors shall be prepared every May listing the turnover per year, and each job category over the last three years. A report from the affirmative action officer shall be included in the agenda of the June Board meeting or that meeting closest to June.

6) *Goals and Timetables:* The ACLU shall endeavor to employ within three years of the adoption of this affirmative action plan and thereafter at least 20% minorities and at least 50% women at every level of employment within the ACLU.

To the extent that the ACLU in any one year is more than 50% short of those goals, the ACLU in a good faith effort to meet its affirmative action goals, shall fill at least half of its open positions at each respective level of employment with minorities and/or women to the extent that they are under-employed at those levels.

To the extent that the ACLU in any two consecutive years is at least 50%

short of its goals of employing 20% minorities and 50% women at every level of employment within the ACLU, the ACLU in a good faith effort to meet its affirmative action goals shall hire into the next available position at each under-represented employment level a minority and/or a woman to the extent that either minorities or women are under-employed at those levels.

If at the end of two years, the ACLU is more than 50% short of its goals of employing 20% minorities and 50% women at every level of employment within the ACLU, $2,000 shall be allocated for recruitment, as described in Section 8, over and above the amount spent for such purposes in the previous year.

Where specific qualifications are met, hiring will be done on the basis of affirmative action.

7) *Job Descriptions:* The affirmative action officer shall annually review the job descriptions of all non-union positions[1] to ensure that there are no non-job-related requirements. All job advertisements shall conform to the job description which has been approved by the affirmative action officer and shall be reviewed by said officer before being placed.

8) *Recruitment:* The ACLU shall develop the tools necessary to carry out a program of affirmative action recruitment. Lists should be developed and regularly updated of organizations and publications most likely to reach those minorities and women who might be interested in employment within the ACLU. These organizations and publications shall annually be provided with a copy of the ACLU Affirmative Action Plan, and should receive employment announcements for each job opening in the ACLU at least one month in advance of interviewing for positions paying under $17,000/year and two months in advance of interviewing for jobs paying $17,000/year and over. ACLU Board and National Advisory Committee members shall also receive such employment announcements.

Interviewing minority and women applicants may require that they be provided transportation so they may be interviewed in New York or that those responsible for ACLU hiring travel to the geographical residence of the applicants. The ACLU budget shall include an allocation for this purpose.

9) *Grievances:* For employees not covered by the clerical union contract, any complaint arising under this Affirmative Action Plan against the ACLU or any of its employees shall be reviewed by the affirmative action officer, the executive director, the complainant and his or her representative. If resolution of the complaint is not reached within three weeks of the notice of the complaint, the complainant may request a hearing before a Hearing Committee made up of three members of the Board of Directors, one chosen by the complainant, one by the executive director, and one by the first two. The Hearing Committee shall recommend disposition, which shall be final.

Grievances of employees covered by the union contract shall be handled in accordance with the collective bargaining agreement.

---

[1] This refers to positions not covered by the collective bargaining contract with clerical employees.

The executive director and associate director shall bargain with the union in an effort to have affirmative action complaints referred to the affirmative action officer as an additional remedy for union employees. [Board Minutes, September 24-25, 1977.]

***

(b) *Personnel Policies*

Terms of Employment

1) *Executive Director:* The Board of Directors is responsible for hiring and firing of the executive director. The executive director serves at the pleasure of the Board of Directors.

2) *Senior Staff:* The associate director, the legal director and the Washington Office director are employed and may be removed by the executive director with the concurrence of the Executive Committee.

3) *Other Staff:* The executive director is responsible for all other hiring and firing of national staff. While ultimate responsibility for such hiring and firing remains with the executive director, of course, he or she may delegate this authority as he or she sees fit.

An employee covered by this section may be terminated after written notice which shall be given at least 15 days in advance of termination. The employee may receive 15 days pay in lieu of the 15-day notice. If requested by the employee, a written statement of the job-related reasons for termination shall be supplied. The employee shall be entitled to a hearing. The hearing shall be by a committee constituted as set out hereafter. The employee's request for a hearing shall be filed with the executive director no more than 30 days after receipt of the notice of termination. The executive director shall notify the chair of the request.

The Hearing Committee shall be made up of these members of the Board of Directors, one chosen by the employee, one chosen by the executive director and the third chosen by the first two. The executive director and the employee shall make appointments to the Hearing Committee within 5 days of receipt of the request for hearing by the executive director. Those two shall select the third member within 48 hours of the appointment of the second member.

Time is of the essence. The date for hearing shall be set promptly and the hearing shall take place no later than one week after the date the committee has been constituted. The employee shall be entitled to one adjournment upon request. No other adjournments shall be had unless mutually agreed upon.

The executive director shall have the burden of persuading the committee that the termination was for job-related reasons.

Decisions of the committee, which shall be based upon evidence adduced at the hearing, shall be final. All records pertaining to termination shall be confidential unless confidentiality is waived by the employee.

4) *Terminations for Budgetary Reasons:* An employee laid off because of budgetary considerations shall have first priority for rehiring if that position is

refunded within three months. An employee believing the budgetary considerations to be spurious may challenge their validity before a Hearing Committee established pursuant to the provisions of Section 3 above. The hearing shall be for the purpose of establishing that the termination was budget-related.

5) *Term of Employment:* At the time of employment, the employee shall be informed as to whether or not the position is for a specific term, or dependent upon a limited funding authorization, or otherwise of limited duration.

6) *Severance Pay:* All new employees and all employees with more than one year of national office service whose employment is involuntarily terminated (for reasons other than such employee's misconduct) shall be entitled to one week severance pay for each full year or fraction thereof of national office service, up to a maximum of 16 weeks severance pay. [Board Minutes, December 3-4, 1977.]

This section does not apply to employees employed for specific terms or limited duration, as provided in Section 5.

Employees terminated during their first year for reasons other than such employees' misconduct shall be entitled to two weeks notice.

7) *Recruitment:* In seeking qualified candidates for filling vacant positions covered by this agreement, first priority shall be given to affirmative action recruitment. Career development recruitment from within the ACLU and the affiliates shall be encouraged.

8) *Job Descriptions:* Every position shall be covered by a written job description which includes the responsibilities and tasks to be performed, the minimum and optimum qualifications for the job, and the salary range. Any other pertinent conditions, such as part-time or temporary nature of the job, overtime or compensatory time provisions shall also be included.

9) *Part-Time Employment and Other Employment Arrangements:* Part-time, shared-time, and by-the-hour work contracts may be arranged by mutual agreement and shall be encouraged. Any person working regularly twenty or more hours per week and otherwise eligible shall receive benefits, vacation, and all other prerequisites of employment in an amount proportionate to the average number of hours worked per week.

10) *Benefits:* The executive director shall propose what benefits shall be provided to staff. The Executive Committee shall approve benefit coverage or changes therein, reporting such in its minutes to the Board.[1]

11) *Vacations:* Vacation entitlement schedules shall from time to time be established in advance by the executive director with the concurrence of the Executive Committee. The schedule approved on October 1, 1977 entitles each employee to 22 vacation days per year. Employees working for less than one year shall be entitled to vacation time on a pro-rata basis. Vacation time shall

---

[1] The Executive Committee approved on October 29, 1977, and April 29, 1978, a benefit schedule for national ACLU staff. If you wish to see the benefits schedule, please contact Alan Reitman at the national office.

not be accumulated from year to year except on exceptional circumstances approved in advance by the executive director. In no event shall more than 3 years' vacation time be accumulated.

12) *Sabbaticals:* Employees are entitled to sabbaticals of three months with full pay after seven years employment. This policy is retroactive until seven years prior to October 1, 1977. Therefore, those employees who already have seven years of service are entitled to sabbaticals, but do not have credit for additional sabbaticals based on service of more than seven years.

This section shall apply to national office service. Employees joining the national ACLU staff after affiliate service shall receive half credit for the period on affiliate staff.

Except with the permission of the executive director, no more than one member of the staff may take a sabbatical at any given time in order of seniority. In the event that the executive director believes that the time a particular staff person chooses for a sabbatical is inconvenient for the ACLU, the executive director may require a postponement not to exceed nine months.

13) *Evaluation, Personnel Files:* Every employee shall have an annual review of her/his job performance by both her/his supervisor, to have such reviews entered into her/his personnel file, to view her/his personnel file, and to challenge any materials included therein and to note on any such materials which remain in the file that they have been challenged.

14) *Relations Between Board of Directors and Employees:* Members of the Board of Directors wishing to complain about or on behalf of an employee should go to the executive director. If the response is considered inadequate, then the complaint may be brought to the Executive Committee.

15) *Grievance Procedure:* The Executive Committee established, and the Board approved, a grievance procedure for those covered by this document.

Grievances of employees not covered by Section 3 of this personnel policy or the Affirmative Action Plan of ACLU shall be dealt with in the following manner:

a) An employee having a grievance against his/her supervisor shall first seek to resolve the grievance by informal discussion with his/her supervisor.

b) If the employee/supervisor grievance is not resolved, the employee may ask the executive director to resolve it. Both the grievant's and the supervisor's views should be presented in writing.

c) If the matter is not resolved under (b), the employee may bring the matter to the attention of the Executive Committee for final resolution.

d) An employee having a grievance against the executive director may ask the chairman to resolve it. Both the grievant's and the executive director's views should be presented in writing. If not satisfied with the chairman's decision, the employee or the executive director can bring the issue to the Executive Committee for final resolution.

e) An employee having a general grievance, unrelated to his/her supervisor or the executive director, shall bring the grievance to the attention of the executive director. If not satisfied with the executive director's decision, he/she may ask the chairman to resolve it.

16) *Collective Bargaining Agreement:* The executive director is responsible for negotiation and implementation of collective bargaining agreements with union personnel.

17) *Time Sequence of Provisions Adopted:* The provisions here approved will become automatically operative 90 days from this date, providing that the executive director will consult with representatives of the staff covered hereunder and will report back to the Board any serious reservations or disagreement of such staff to the approved provisions. The staff shall be able to review the materials the executive director supplies to the Board and to make recommendations to the Board and the Executive Committee concerning them. Further, the Executive Committee shall set operative times for the matters referred to them and report all their actions to the Board. The staff shall be consulted on the matters considered by the Executive Committee. [Board Minutes, June 18-19, 1977.]

SUPPLEMENTARY MATERIAL TO FURTHER
INFORMATION (not policy) SECTION

The *1976 Policy Guide* included a section headed Further Information (not policy) after certain policies. This section contained background information on key Supreme Court decisions, national legislation, and, in some instances, important lower-court decisions and state legislative actions. It was felt that this procedure would assist the reader by providing factual information that places the individual policy in a current context.

The *1977 Supplement* continues this practice by 1) updating and including revisions and deletions for certain policies and 2) introducing new Further Information (not policy) material. The section below covers the items described in 1) and 2) above and should be read after consulting the actual ACLU policy in the original *Guide*. In a few instances, for reasons of editorial clarification, new Further Information (not policy) material has been integrated with the policies in the *Supplement*.

FREEDOM OF BELIEF, EXPRESSION, AND ASSOCIATION

Access to the Media   *Policy #11*

In *Miami Herald Publishing Co. v. Tornillo* (1974), the Supreme Court held a Florida "right to reply" statute granting a political candidate equal space to reply to criticism by a newspaper to be an unconstitutional infringement on freedom of the press. The Court equated forcing the newspaper to publish that which "reason" dictates with a command forbidding newspapers to publish specified matters. In *Columbia Broadcasting System, Inc. v. Democratic National Committee* (1973), it was held that there is no right of access to broadcasting facilities for paid editorial advertisements under First Amendment or the "fairness doctrine." The Supreme Court reversed the District of Columbia Court of Appeals decision which held that if a station accepts some paid advertising, a ban on public issue advertisements would violate the First Amendment.

News Media Sources and Information   *Policy #12*

In *Branzburg v. Hayes,* (1972), the Supreme Court held that the First Amendment does not relieve a newspaper reporter of his or her obligation to testify before a grand jury in response to a subpoena. The Court found no First Amendment testimonial immunity for journalists to withhold facts or sources of evidence relevant to a grand jury's investigation. The need for effective grand jury investigations was found to "override the consequential but uncertain burden on news gathering" and the likely inhibition of confidential sources of

149

information. The Court found that such testimony by journalists would not result in a "significant constriction of the flow of news to the public."

The Supreme Court struck down a pre-trial gag order in *Nebraska Press Association v. Stuart* (1976) where it could find no evidence that alternatives to such an order would not have sufficiently protected the rights of the accused and where it could not be clearly shown that the order would have in fact provided such protection. The order prohibited the publication of confessions, admissions and other facts "strongly implicative" of the defendant prior to the empaneling of a jury in a trial for multiple murder. The Court found that as applied to information derived from public judicial proceedings, the order was clearly invalid. As the information obtained from law enforcement officers or third parties, it was held that the heavy burden of justification for imposing a prior restraint had not been met.

Commercial Advertising   *Policy #15*

In *Bigelow v. Virginia* (1975), the Supreme Court began to significantly erode the doctrine that commercial speech is outside the purview of the First Amendment. The Court looked to whether the public interest in the commercial speech outweighs the state's need for regulation. In *Bigelow,* an advertisement for abortions resulted in the conviction of the managing editor of a newspaper under a Virginia statute prohibiting the dissemination of information encouraging abortion. The Court held the statute unconstitutional and reasoned that although commercial speech may be treated differently, and states may have greater latitude in its regulation, the Court would look to the public interest in the commercial speech, in this case the constitutional right to abortion, to determine the degree of First Amendment protection to be afforded.

In *Virginia State Bd. of Pharmacy v. Virginia Citizens' Consumer Council, Inc.* (1976), the Court held that commercial advertising is entitled to some protection even if it does not pertain to the exercise of some other constitutional right as was the case in *Bigelow.* Protection is to be afforded both the source and the recipient of such communications reasoned the Court, in striking down a Virginia law which prohibited the advertising of prescription drug prices. Consumers were found to have a First Amendment right to receive this information, and thus had standing to sue. Again, the Court noted that commercial speech could be subject to more extensive regulation concerning time, place, manner and the making of false statements.

In the recent case of *Linmark Associates v. Town of Willingboro, N.J.* (1977), a township ordinance which forbade the posting of "for sale" and "sold" signs was declared unconstitutional even though its purpose was to stem or prevent "white flight" and the ordinance precluded only one particular form of communication. The Court held that it impaired the flow of truthful and legitimate commercial information and noted that the ordinance was unnecessary to achieve its objective.

In *Bates v. State Bar of Arizona* (1977), the Supreme Court struck down a state bar association rule prohibiting the advertising of the prices of routine legal services. The Court found that such a rule unconstitutionally restricts the flow of information to the public.

Broadcasting Codes *Policy #18*

In 1975 the NAB added to its code a "family viewing" standard. This limits programming, during the first hour of prime time and the immediately preceding hour,[1] to entertainment "appropriate for viewing by a general family audience." The Union's general opposition to codes, as well as the impact of the rule in imposing prior restraints on the content of programming, prompted the ACLU's particular opposition to the family viewing standard. Moreover, the rule appears to have been imposed because of pressures by Congress and the FCC, thus violating the constitutional guarantees that preclude governmental regulation of content of broadcasting.

Late in 1975 a group of writers and producers, including the Writers, Directors and Screen Actors Guilds, and Norman Lear, the producer and creator of several television shows, including "All In The Family," filed suit against the FCC, the networks and the National Association of Broadcasters. In November 1976, in *Writers' Guild of America v. FCC,* the Federal District Court held that the networks and the National Association of Broadcasters violated the First Amendment by adopting the "family hour" viewing provisions of the NAB code in response to pressure by the FCC. Choosing not to pass upon the constitutionality of the "family hour" policy, the court found that both networks and the NAB infringed upon independent licensee programming decisions in violation of the First Amendment, which was held to compel the networks to "program exclusively on the basis of their independent judgment," and thus to independently decide whether or not to adopt a "family hour" guideline.

Curbs on Network Control of Programming *Policy #20*

The FCC has periodically reviewed the provisions of the Prime Time Access Rule. Since the Board voiced its approval for the general concept behind the Prime Time Access Rule, the Commission has made significant changes upon which the Board has not had an opportunity to pass. In September 1975, Prime Time Access Rule III was instituted by the FCC. The revised rule provides that commercial television stations in the top 50 markets shall reserve one of the four hours of prime time for non-network programming. Network programs excluded from the three-hour limit include children's programs, public affairs programs or documentaries, on-the-spot news coverage, political broadcasts by or on behalf of candidates for public office, 30-minute regular network news broadcasts when

---

[1] This time is between 7 and 9 PM except in the Midwest where family viewing applies to the 6 to 8 PM timeslot.

adjacent to a full hour of local news or public affairs programming, runover of live sports events, broadcasts of international sports events (e.g., Olympic Games) New Year's Day college football games and other special network programming which constitutes the entire programming on the network for the same evening.

Transit Radio   *Policy #33*

In *Lehman v. City of Shaker Heights* (1974), the Supreme Court ruled that a municipal policy prohibiting paid political advertisements to be purchased on the public transit system, and thus limiting its advertising to only the commercial and service-oriented variety, was not a violation of the First and Fourteenth Amendment rights of the petitioner, a candidate for public office. The plurality opinion stressed the commercial nature of the transit system, declining to view it as a forum for the communication of ideas. The Court found the risk of imposing upon a "captive audience" to be a reasonable legislative objective.

Government Employees   *Policy #36*

In *United States Civil Service Commission v. National Association of Letter Carriers* (1973) the Supreme Court reaffirmed its 1947 holding, in *United Public Workers v. Mitchell,* that the Hatch Act prohibition of political activity by federal employee is constitutional. The Court reasoned that there is no absolute right to political association nor to engage in political activity. These rights are regulated in other contexts; and the government interest in insuring that federal service is based on meritorious performance rather than political service and in seeing that laws are impartially executed justifies such governmental regulation.

The 1968 decision in *Pickering v. Board of Education* concerned the dismissal of a school teacher for his publication of a letter critical of certain school board policies. The Supreme Court said: "Teachers are as a class the members of a community most likely to have informed and definite opinions as to how funds allotted to the operations of the schools should be spent. Accordingly it is essential that they be able to speak out freely on such questions without fear of retaliatory dismissal."

The 1974 case of *Arnett et al v. Kennedy et al* concerned the discharge of a non-probationary federal employee of the Office of Economic Opportunity after his supervisor had given him written notice of the charges against him, including the charge that the employee had publicly stated that the supervisor and his assistant had attempted to bribe a third party. The employee asserted that he had a right to a pre-termination hearing, and that his statements were protected by the First Amendment. The discharge was affected pursuant to the provisions of the Lloyd-La Follette Act. The Federal District Court in Illinois held that the Act and attendant administrative regulations violated due process requirements in failing to provide for a pre-termination hearing, and that the statute was unconstitutionally vague in failing to furnish sufficiently precise guidelines as to what kind of speech could be made the basis for a removal action.

The Supreme Court reversed the decision, holding that the discharge procedures established under the Act did not violate due process rights and the Act was not unconstitutionally vague or overbroad.

In *Elrod v. Burns* (1976), the Court held that the politically motivated discharge of public employees was a proper question for the courts in that it raised First and Fourteenth Amendment issues. The employees had brought suit alleging First and Fourteenth Amendment violations in their discharge on the sole ground that they were not affiliated with the political party of the present sheriff. Neither the political question doctrine nor separation of powers rendered the claim inappropriate for judicial resolution. The Court further held that such patronage dismissals would violate the First Amendment in making relinquishment of the right to political association the price of holding a public job. Issuance of a preliminary injunction was proper given the showing of irreparable injury and of probable success on the merits.

The Armed Forces   *Policy #38*

In *Parker v. Levy* (1974), the Supreme Court rejected Captain Howard Levy's claims that two articles of the Uniform Code of Military Justice were so vague as to deny due process or so overbroad as to unconstitutionally burden free speech. Articles 133 and 134 of the Code proscribe "conduct unbecoming an officer and a gentleman" and "all disorders and neglects to the prejudice of good order and discipline in the armed forces." As an army doctor stationed in South Carolina, Levy's claims arose from a court-martial because of statements made during his hospital rounds to the effect that the Vietnam war was wrong and that black soldiers should refuse to serve there.

Secondary School Students' Civil Liberties   *Policy #69*

In the case of *Tinker v. Des Moines School District* (1969), the Supreme Court held the wearing of black armbands by high school students as a symbolic protest against the Vietnam war a legitimate exercise of expression, protected by the First Amendment. The Court noted that neither "students [n]or teachers shed the constitutional rights to freedom of speech or expression at the school house gate."

In *Goss v. Lopez* (1975), the Court found that the suspension of a public school student for even one day raised a due process issue. Some due process was deemed to be required from the school administration because such an exclusion from the educational process infringes upon both liberty and property interests and thus mandates constitutional review. Four weeks after *Goss* in *Wood v.*

Strickland (1975), the Supreme Court held school board members and school officials personally liable for intentional violations of students' constitutional rights. However, in a retreat from the previous trend toward expanding constitutional safeguards of public school students, the Court held in *Ingraham v. Wright* (1977), that the paddling of public school students does not constitute cruel and unusual punishment in violation of the Eighth Amendment. The decision further held that the due process clause does not require notice and an opportunity to be heard prior to the administration of corporal punishment.

Bus Transportation, Textbooks, Other Services   *Policy #73*

In the past few years the Supreme Court has lent increasing support to the ACLU position by invalidating a variety of state attempts to provide aid to non-public schools as violative of the no-establishment of religion clause. The cases include statutes attempting to provide "auxiliary services" to parochial school pupils, *Meek v. Pittenger* (1975); *Levitt v. Committee for Public Education* (1973); salary supplements to non-public school teachers, *Lemon v. Kurtzman* (1971); funds for maintenance and repair of facilities, tuition reimbursement, and tax benefits for parents of children attending non-public schools, *Committee for Public Education v. Nyquist* (1973), *Sloan v. Lemon* (1973); instructional material and equipment and field trips, *Wolman v. Walter* (1977); reimbursement for recordkeeping and testing services required by state law, *New York v. Cathedral Academy* (1977).

However, in *Board of Education v. Allen* (1968), the Supreme Court refused to invalidate on its face a New York statute providing for the lending of textbooks to children in religious schools. It also reaffirmed that ruling in *Meek v. Pittenger* and in *Wolman v. Walter* (1977). In *Wolman,* the Supreme Court upheld a statute authorizing state finding of the standardized tests and scoring services used in the public schools, diagnostic services on non-public school premises, and therapeutic and remedial services rendered to non-public school students off the premises of non-public schools.

Higher Education   *Policy #79*

The Supreme Court has upheld both state and federal aid to institutions of higher education against challenges that such aid violates the "no establishment of religion" clause. A South Carolina law providing funds for the financing of projects at colleges was ruled to have a secular purpose in that it did not apply solely to religiously-affiliated institutions, and was held not to advance or inhibit religion because of the non-pervasive nature of religion at the institutions and because the funds were not to be used for any specifically religious function. *Hunt v. McNair* (1973). In *Roemer v. Board of Public Work of Maryland* (1976), the Supreme Court upheld annual non-categorical grants to four Catholic colleges. The Court found that, even though religion or theology courses were required and many classes were begun with prayer, the colleges were not pervasively sectarian.

Grants to sectarian colleges under the Federal Higher Education Facilities Act of 1963 were upheld by the Supreme Court in *Tilton v. Richardson* (1971) on the ground that it had not been shown that religion permeated the secular education of the colleges involved and because the aid was in the form of one-time-only payments for religiously neutral facilities, thus avoiding entanglement of religion problems. Moreover, even as to these grants, the Court invalidated a provision in the statute which, after 20 years, would have freed facilities aided under its terms from the prohibition of use for sectarian purposes.

Military Chaplaincy   *Policy #80*

In *Anderson v. Laird* (1972), the United States Court of Appeals for the District of Columbia Circuit held that the requirement of mandatory chapel attendance for cadets and midshipmen at three federal military academies violates the establishment clause.

Church Political Activities   *Policy #88*

In *McDaniel v. Paty* (1977), a minister has challenged a provision of the Tennessee constitution which precludes ministers and priests of all denominations from serving in the state legislature. A call for a limited constitutional convention established the same qualifications for delegate as those for membership in the state House of Representatives and thus included the above provision. The minister has contended that such a provision offends the free exercise and establishment clause, is unconstitutionally vague, and violates the equal protection clause in denying him the right to vote and the right to be a candidate for public office. The Tennessee Supreme Court has held that the provision offends neither the free exercise nor the establishment clause. The Supreme Court agreed to hear the case, and a decision should be forthcoming.

Conscientious Objection   *Policy #112*

In *Welsh v. United States* (1970) the Supreme Court reversed the draft evasion conviction of a man whose opposition to war was not based upon a religious belief. His opposition was based, instead, upon the registrant's conscientious scruples against participation in any war and his belief that killing was morally wrong, although these beliefs were not "religious" in the traditional sense. The Court agreed that the proper test was whether the person's opposition to war stemmed from moral, ethical or religious beliefs about right or wrong, provided that such beliefs are held with the strength of traditional religious convictions.

The claim of a draft registrant who refused military service because of objection to a particular war, *viz.* the Viet Nam War, but not to war in general, was rejected by the Supreme Court in *Gillette v. United States* (1971). The Court said that a proper construction of a section of the Selective Service Act delineating the standard for conscientious objections to military service required such a conclusion. The Court rejected the argument that such a construction violated the "free exercise of religion" clause of the First Amendment.

In *Johnson v. Robison* (1974), the Supreme Court upheld the denial of educational benefits under the Veterans' Readjustment Benefits Act to a conscientious objector who performed alternative civilian service. The Court rejected his claims that the denial of benefits violated his right to equal protection of the laws and his right to free exercise of religion.

Amnesty   *Policy #114*

American military involvement in Southeast Asia essentially ended on March 28, 1973 when the last forces left the area. By Executive Proclamation 4313 (September 16, 1974) President Ford introduced a "clemency program" providing for "earned re-entry" for limited classes of draft violators, military deserters and veterans with less-than-honorable discharges from military service.

The ACLU sharply criticized the assumptions and implications of this program, which ended on September 15, 1975. The government program had processed approximately 22,000 clemency applications, out of an estimated 750,000 persons in need of amnesty. It had given most of those applicants irrelevant or inadequate remedies in exchange for periods of alternative service.

On January 21, 1977, President Carter announced the pardon of Vietnam War resisters. The pardon was unconditional and applied to all persons convicted of violations of the Selective Service Laws, unless the Attorney General felt that a serious act of violence warranted continued prosecution. The President's action also required the dismissal with prejudice of pending indictments, the halt to pending investigations, releases of those in custody or on probation or parole, prohibition of the opening of new investigations, and termination of alternative service requirements incurred by those who participated in the previous President Ford clemency program. The Carter pardon has been defined by the Attorney General to include draft card burning, "continuing offenses" (such as non-registration), and bail-jumping charges which occurred at any stage of a draft law prosecution.

On March 28, 1977, the Department of Defenses (DOD) announced a Special Discharge Review Program (SDRP) for Vietnam-era veterans with general and undesirable discharges, absentees still at large and some clemency discharges. The SDRP provided that Vietnam-era absentees may return, have charges against them dismissed, and be given an other-than-honorable discharge by reason of prolonged absences if non-absence related charges are also pending. The SDRP provided for a case-by-case review if an eligible Vietnam-era veteran applied by October 4, 1977. Taking advantage of the weak support the Administration gave the SDRP, the program was attacked by Congress when both houses prohibited the DOD from spending funds on paid advertising of the program. Congress then passed an amendment to prohibit the use of Veterans' Administration funds for benefits for those who have had the military discharge upgraded from undesirable under President Carter's review program even if the veteran would have gotten an upgrade under the normal proceedings. This compromise permitted payment of benefits after a new review and rejected an absolute ban passed by the House.

The ACLU has criticized the Carter Administration for failure to veto S.1307 (Public Law 95-126). One of the most obnoxious provisions of the statute is that it creates a new bar to Veteran Administration benefits (a 180 day AWOL) which denies benefits *only* to veterans who received upgrades of their undesirable discharges under the SDRP program or who, in the future, receive upgrades under any program. This aspect of the law denies equal protection of the law to poor and uneducated Vietnam-era veterans who learned belatedly of a review system. Those who were well-counselled received relief in 75% of the cases even before the SDRP. The Union is challenging this provision of P.L. 95-126.

DUE PROCESS OF LAW

Search and Arrest   *Policy #201*

In recent years the Supreme Court has eroded the Fourth Amendment's protections against unreasonable arrests and searches. Expanding on the "stop and frisk" doctrine that ACLU argued against a decade ago, the Court has ruled that such law enforcement investigatory activity can be based on the flimsiest of information and can justify a consequent arrest and search without a warrant. *Adams v. Williams* (1972). The Court has similarly said that persons stopped and cited for minor traffic offenses could be subjected to full-blown personal searches on the basis of such arrests, and that the fruits of such searches can be used in evidence. *United States v. Robinson* (1973).

In *United States v. Edwards* (1973), the Court upheld the warrantless seizure of a defendant's clothing even though ten hours had elapsed since the time of the lawful arrest. In *United States v. Watson* (1976), the Court held that the warrantless arrest of an individual in a public place upon probable cause did not violate the Fourth Amendment. Subsequently, the notion of "public place" was extended in *United States v. Santana* (1976), in which the warrantless arrest of a person standing in the doorway of her home was upheld and used as the basis to search the premises for contraband.

A recent case, however, represents a departure from the Burger Court's conservative stance toward search and seizure issues. In *United States v. Chadwick* (1977), the Court ruled that the warrantless search of a footlocker, seized from the open trunk of a parked car, violated the Fourth Amendment. Noting that the contents of the luggage were not open to public view, the Court refused to extend the rationale underlying automobile searches to this case.

Interrogation and Arraignment   *Policy #203*

Since the *Miranda* case, Supreme Court decisions have cut back on the reach of that landmark ruling. *In Harris v. New York* (1971), the Court held that statements inadmissible because obtained without *Miranda* warnings could nevertheless be used to attack the defendant's credibility if the defendant took the stand to testify in his or her own defense. In *Oregon v. Hass* (1975), the Court held that a statement, taken shortly after the defendant requested a lawyer, could also be used for impeachment purposes. In *Oregon v. Mathiason* (1977) the Court held that *Miranda* warnings need not be given to a defendant who voluntarily entered the stationhouse and made a confession in response to police questioning. *Brewer v. Williams* (1977) represents an undisguised attempt to overturn the *Miranda* ruling. The Court declined the invitation, however, holding that where judicial proceedings had begun and an agreement had been reached with the defendant's attorney that no interrogation would take place, the defendant's right to counsel was violated by the police officer's attempt to solicit information.

There has been one step forward. A suspect's silence, following *Miranda* warnings, cannot be used against him or her at trial, *United States v. Hale* (1975). In *Doyle v. Ohio* (1976), the Supreme Court resolved a question that had been left open in *United States v. Hale*. At trial, the prosecutor attempted to cross-examine two defendants about their failure to tell an exculpatory story at the time of arrest. The Supreme Court held that the limited use of the defendant's post-arrest silence for impeaching the witnesses' testimony violates the due process clause.

In 1969, the system of United States Commissioners was abolished by an act of Congress and replaced by United States Magistrates. The magistrates do have fixed salaries and must be members of the bar.

Marijuana   *Policy #214*

A landmark decision of the United States Court of Appeals for the Sixth Circuit declared Ohio's minimum penalties for sale and possession of marijuana to be so excessive and disproportionate to the offense as to violate the Eighth

Amendment. *Downey v. Perini* (1975). Similarly, a Federal District Court in Virginia held that a sentence of 40 years and $20,000 in fines for the defendant's possession with intent to distribute and distribution of less than 9 ounces of marijuana constituted cruel and unusual punishment under the Eighth Amendment, *David v. Zahradnick* (1977).

One state Supreme Court (Alaska) has declared that the constitutional right of privacy extends to the possession and use of marijuana in one's own home. *Ravin v. State,* (1975). However, the United States Supreme Court subsequently refused to review the dismissal by the Federal District Court in Louisiana of a similar case. The dismissal was based on the grounds that the privacy argument in support of the right to smoke marijuana did not present a substantial federal question since the allegations were "plainly without merit." *Louisiana Affiliate of the National Organization for the Reform of Marijuana Laws (NORML) v. Guste* (1975).

While the ACLU favors decriminalization of the possession, use, and sale of marijuana, it recognizes as an important interim step citation laws recently adopted in ten states (Oregon, Alaska, Maine, Colorado, California, Ohio, Minnesota, Mississippi, New York, North Carolina) which treat the possession of small amounts of marijuana similar to a minor traffic violation. Under these laws the offender receives a summons similar to a traffic ticket and is subject to a small fine; he or she is not subject to arrest or imprisonment nor is he or she left with a permanent criminal record. Laws of this kind will serve to greatly reduce the nearly half million marijuana arrests now occurring annually in this country, more than 90% of which are for possession of small amounts of the drug.

Counsel for Indigents, Minorities, and   *Policy #218*
Unpopular Individuals

In 1974 Congress created a Legal Services Corporation to operate legal services programs previously controlled by the Office of Economic Opportunity. Congress amended the Legal Services Corporation Act in 1977 to extend appropriations for the following three fiscal years. The 1977 amendments left intact the Corporation's basic structure and made only a few changes of any significance.

The Corporation will continue to be governed by an 11-member Board of Directors appointed by the President. The 1977 Amendments specify, however, that the Board membership shall include eligible clients and be "generally representative of the organized bar, attorneys providing legal assistance to eligible clients, and the general public."

Staff attorneys are subject to the Hatch Act and to a specific prohibition against running for partisan political office.

The Amendments retain, and in some cases strengthen, various restrictions on the use of funds made available to the Corporation. Funds may not be used, for example, to support or conduct a training program to advocate particular public policies or to encourage political activities, labor or anti-labor activities, boycotts, picketing, strikes, and demonstrations.

The Amendments further restrict legal services attorneys from engaging in legislative-related services for their clients, by adding "state proposals by initiative petition" to the list of legislative and executive actions which the attorneys are prevented from influencing.

The ACLU successfully opposed a House provision which would have prohibited legal assistance with respect to any gay rights issues. Despite ACLU opposition, however, the existing prohibition against the use of Corporation funds for school desegregation litigation was retained.

Although the ACLU always has supported the concept of federal legal services, the Union consistently has opposed these kinds of restrictions on the activities of staff attorneys and the use of Corporation funds. The ACLU believes that legal services attorneys should be able to perform the same services for their clients that private attorneys provide for theirs.

Contempt of Court Trial   *Policy #224*

In *Taylor v. Hayes* (1974), where the Union filed an *amicus curiae* brief, and in *Codispoti v. Pennsylvania* (1974), the Supreme Court adopted most of the standards set forth in ACLU policy on summary punishment for contempt of court.

However, the Court has taken a severe approach in determining when these procedural safeguards will apply. In *United States v. Wilson* (1975), the Court held that summary punishment could be imposed against witnesses who are granted immunity during a trial but refuse to testify on Fifth Amendment self-incrimination grounds. Although the refusals to testify were non-violent and respectful, the Court stated that such intentional obstructions of the trial's progress were so "disruptive" as to exempt the contempt sanction from the notice and hearing requirements set forth in *Federal Rules of Criminal Procedure* 42(b).

Privilege Against Self-Incrimination   *Policy #240*

The privilege against self-incrimination suffered a major setback in *Kastigar v. United States* (1972) and *Zicarelli v. New Jersey State Commissioner of Investigation* (1972). The cases concerned the Organized Crime Control Act of 1970 which cut to the heart of the Fifth Amendment privilege by providing that a witness claiming the privilege could nevertheless be compelled to testify by being granted "use" immunity, i.e., his or her testimony or evidence derived from such testimony could not be utilized, but the witness could still be prosecuted for any crimes admitted in the testimony, so long as independent evidence was used against the witness. That limited "use" immunity was a substitute for the broader, historically approved "transactional" immunity which required that a witness had to be granted *complete* immunity from prosecution before being compelled to incriminate himself or herself.

The Union joined the attack on the Act, arguing that the Fifth Amendment meant that a person had an absolute right to remain silent and could never at all be legally compelled to incriminate himself or herself, that the requirement of transactional immunity was the minimum constitutional compromise which could justify displacing that right of silence, and that the Act was accordingly unconstitutional. The Supreme Court disagreed, holding that use immunity was "coexistensive with the privilege" against self-incrimination.

In a related area, the Court has also held that compelling a grand jury witness to furnish voice samples did not violate the Fifth Amendment since the purpose of the privilege against self-incrimination was only to protect against "testimonial" or "communicative" statements. *United States v. Dionisio* (1973). The Court has said the same is true for handwriting samples. *United States v. Mara* (1973).

In the context of grand juries the Court has not recognized witnesses' claims of self-incrimination. The plurality opinion in *United States v. Mandujano* (1976), stated that *Miranda* warnings need not be given to a grand jury witness who was called to testify about his own possible involvement in criminal activities.

In *Cupp v. Murphy* (1973), police at the stationhouse took fingernail scrapings from the defendant without placing him under formal arrest or obtaining a search warrant. Although the Court recognized that this intrusion went beyond the "mere physical characteristics exposed to the public" in *Dionisio* and *Mara,* the limited search was nonetheless upheld because of the destructibility of the evidence.

The government's seizure of incriminating business records, whether obtained in the defendant's office or the office of his or her attorney, does not violate the Fifth Amendment privilege against self-incrimination since the parties are not "witnesses" and are not "compelled" to testify, *Fisher v. United States* (1976) and *Andresen v. Maryland* (1976).

Ombudsman   *Policy #243*

The states of Alaska, Hawaii, Iowa and Nebraska have official ombudsmen, as do a few local communities and departments of municipalities. In general, the ombudsman idea has not caught on.

Electronic Evesdropping   *Policy #249*

In 1968 Congress passed a law permitting wiretapping for 30-day periods, if judicial warrants were issued upon probable cause that a tap would produce evidence of a particular crime specified in the law. The ACLU has opposed this statute as unconstitutional and its permissive provisions have not yet been upheld against full constitutional attack.

With respect to warrantless wiretapping, the Supreme Court has held that such taps violate the Fourth Amendment, although it has left open the question whether a warrantless tap installed on a person or organization "directed and controlled" by a foreign power is also unconstitutional. There are now in the courts a variety of cases brought by the ACLU on behalf of persons suing governmental officials for damages based on warrantless wiretapping.

Mail Covers   *Policy #251*

In 1975 the ACLU won an important decision in the United States Court of Appeals for the Second Circuit granting a New Jersey high school student standing to challenge a FBI mail cover. The mail cover, the court held, violated the First and Fourth Amendments. The case involved a girl who had written the Socialist Workers Party to obtain information about the Party for a term paper she had been assigned to write. As a result of the FBI mail cover on the SWP, she came to the attention of the Newark FBI office which conducted a "national security" investigation of her, including several interviews with her teachers. But in *U.S. v. Leonard* (1975), the same Court of Appeals held that the IRS's mail cover of airmail envelopes without return addresses, mailed from Switzerland to New York, was not in violation of a postal regulation. This regulation authorized mail covers to obtain information regarding the commission or attempted commission of a crime, in spite of the fact that the IRS was not engaged in an investigation of a possible loss of tax revenues through use of secret Swiss bank accounts.

Abortion   *Policy #258*

A woman's right to an abortion was declared part of the constitutionally guaranteed right to privacy in the Supreme Court decision in *Roe v. Wade* (1973). The Court held that during the first trimester of pregnancy any interest the state might have in the woman's health or in protecting fetal life was outweighed by the woman's right to privacy. Therefore the state could not regulate the abortion decision or its implementation at any time during this first trimester except to require that the procedure be done by a physician. From the end of the first trimester until viability the state can regulate abortions in ways reasonably related to protecting maternal health, but it cannot prohibit abortions. After viability the state can prohibit abortions except when necessary to protect the woman's health or life.

In *Doe v. Bolton* (1973) the Court reviewed the constitutionality of state restrictions on abortion. The Court ruled that requiring medical committee approval, concurrence of other physicians, imposing residency and hospital accreditation requirements for abortions were unconstitutional. The Court affirmed the principle that the abortion decision in the first trimester of pregnancy is between the woman and her doctor.

Under the Supreme Court's ruling in *Bigelow v. Virginia* (1975) states cannot prohibit abortion advertisements or the dissemination of information regarding abortion as such actions are violative of the First Amendment. The Court ruled that abortion was an issue upon which there was a great deal of public concern and that the exchange of information on the subject served a valid purpose.

In 1977, the Supreme Court announced decisions in three cases which severely limited the right of low income women to choose to have an abortion, a right supposedly guaranteed to all women in *Roe v. Wade.* In *Maher v. Roe* (1977), the Court held that states participating in the Medicaid program which refuse to pay the expenses incident to non-therapeutic abortions while paying the expenses incident to childbirth do not violate the equal protection rights of women who desire to have abortions. In *Beal v. Roe* (1977), the Court found that the exclusion of non-therapeutic abortions was not "unreasonable" under Title XIX of the Social Security Act which requires state Medicaid plans to establish "reasonable standards" for medical care. Finally, in *Poelker v. Doe* (1977), the Court held that public hospitals do not violate the equal protection clause by providing publicly financed hospital services and facilities for child-birth without providing similar services and facilities for non-therapeutic abortions.

Presently, the Reproductive Freedom Project of the ACLU is involved in *Califano v. McRae,* a suit challenging the constitutionality of the Hyde Amendment on the grounds of equal protection, vagueness (of the language "life endangering" and "medically necessary"), and First Amendment freedom of religion, both with respect to impermissible establishment of religion and to entanglement of church and state.

Two recent Supreme Court cases have dealt with the issue of consent to abortion. In *Planned Parenthood of Central Missouri v. Danforth* (1976), the Supreme Court held that, while an abortion statute may require the written consent of a woman before she has an abortion, and may impose reasonable recordkeeping requirements, it may not require spousal consent, nor may it require the consent of parents of a minor (where the woman is unmarried and under the age of 18). However, in *Bellotti v. Baird* (1976), the Court held that a statute which did not give parents an absolute veto, but rather, required their involvement in the abortion decision, might pass constitutional muster.

Data Collection, Storage and Dissemination   *Policy #267*

The rights of access, amendment, explanation, and knowledge of procedures and remedies suggested in 1-4 above have, with respect to federal agency data banks, been enacted into law. The 1966 Freedom of Information Act and the 1974 Privacy Act give individuals the right to see most personal data about them which is maintained in federal agency record systems. The Privacy Act further affords the right to amend inaccurate, untimely, incomplete or irrelevant information, and certain procedural protections against the disclosure of personal information to other agencies or individuals. In addition, the Privacy Act places upon the data collection activities of federal agencies certain restrictions on the uses of personal information for purposes other than those originally intended when the information was collected, and requires that agencies keep an account of all disclosures of personal information they make to other agencies or individuals. The Act provides judicial as well as administrative remedies.

The "code of fair information practices" embodied in the 1974 Privacy Act does not apply to state and local agencies, nor to private data banks. The 1970 Fair Credit Reporting Act does place some restrictions on credit reporting agencies, and gives the individual the right to learn what information is in his or her credit file, but the Act has no meaningful enforcement mechanism and has not been particularly effective as a protector of privacy. Other than this, there is no federal statutory protection for subjects of privately maintained data banks.

The Privacy Act also limits uses of the Social Security number as a personal identifier by federal, state, and local government agencies (but not private agencies) to uses which were authorized by statute or regulation before January 1, 1975, or to uses authorized by federal legislation after that date.

Attempts to limit governmental access to private data systems have not been particularly successful. For example, the Supreme Court rejected a challenge to the constitutionality of the Bank Secrecy Act, which allows governmental access to the bank records of individuals in *California Bankers Assn. v. Schultz* (1974). And the Supreme Court allowed the Internal Revenue Service to issue "John Doe" summonses to examine the bank records of unspecified individuals who might be liable for taxes in *U.S. v. Bisceglia* (1975).

However, in *U.S. v. Humble Oil and Refining Co.* (1975), the United States Court of Appeals for the Fifth Circuit attempted to limit the scope of *Bisceglia* by holding that the IRS is not authorized to issue "John Doe" summons in aid of research projects or inquiries, when taxpayers or individuals and corporations from whom the information is sought are not the subject of the investigation. The Supreme Court vacated judgment and remanded the case for further consideration in light of *Bisceglia*. On remand, the Court of Appeals held that *Humble Oil* was consistent with *Bisceglia*, and again found that the summons was unauthorized.

EQUALITY BEFORE THE LAW

The 1964 Civil Rights Act forbids discrimination in such public accommodations as hotels, motels, inns, restaurants, cafeterias, lunchrooms, gasoline stations, motion picture houses, theaters, concert halls, sports arenas, stadiums and other places of exhibition and entertainment.

The Supreme Court in two cases has upheld the public accommodations section of the Act. In *Heart of Atlanta Motel v. United States* (1964) the Court concluded that Congress had the power to pass this legislation under the commerce clause of the Constitution. The Court concluded that discrimination by hotels and motels impeded interstate travel by blacks, and thus affected interstate commerce in a manner sufficient to justify passage of the Civil Rights Act. In a companion case, *Katzenbach v. McClung* (1964), the Supreme Court upheld, as a proper exercise of the power granted under the commerce clause, the public accommodations sections as applied to a restaurant receiving about $70,000 worth of food annually that had moved in interstate commerce. The Court said that testimony before both House and Senate committees provided ample basis for the conclusion that interstate travel was obstructed by discrimination by restaurants, that business in general suffered from the discrimination and that many new businesses refrained from locating in areas where discrimination was prevalent. There was a sufficient connection between the discrimination and interstate commerce to support the statute.

Two Supreme Court cases help to show the applicability of the law to facilities not explicitly covered by the statute. In *Daniel v. Paul* (1969) the Court held that a 232-acre area with facilities for swimming, boating, sun bathing, picknicking, miniature golf and dancing was within the coverage of the Act. The Court concluded: 1) the facility was a "place of entertainment" within the meaning of the statute; 2) the facility unquestionably catered to interstate travelers; and 3) a substantial portion of the food served by the snack bar moved in interstate commerce.

In *Tillman v. Wheaton-Haven Recreation Association* (1973) the defendant was an organization formed to operate a swimming pool. Membership was largely confined to residents within a 3/4 mile radius of the pool. When a non-resident member sold his or her property he or she could grant an option of the pool membership to the purchaser. Unlike non-residents, residents of the area required no recommendation for membership, and were given a preference on the waiting list if they applied when the membership limit had been reached. When the policy restricting membership to whites only was challenged, the defendant argued that the facility was a private club and thus not within the purview of the 1964 statute. The Court ruled that there was no selective element for membership other than race. Therefore, the organization was held not to be a private club and its action was prohibited by the statute.

In *Runyon v. McCrary* (1976), the Supreme Court held that the "private club" exemption of the Civil Rights Act of 1964 did not extend to permit private, commercially operated, non-sectarian schools to deny admission to prospective students because they were black, particularly where such schools advertised and offered services to members of the general public and appealed to parents of all children in the area who could meet the academic and admissions requirement.

Education   *Policy #305*

In *Milliken v. Bradley* (1974) the Supreme Court was asked to decide whether a federal court could impose a multi-district, area-wide, remedy to a single district which by law practiced segregation, in the absence of a finding that the districts included in the remedy committed acts which affected segregation in the other districts.

In a 5-4 decision the Court held that before the boundaries of autonomous school districts could be set aside by consolidating separate units for remedial purposes, it must be shown that there has been a constitutional violation in one district that produced a significant segregative effect in another district. The Court indicated that to receive interdistrict relief, the racially discriminatory act of the state or a local school district must have been a substantial cause of the interdistrict segregation. Since the Court did not find that the discriminatory acts of the state and local officials in Detroit had a segregative effect in the separate suburban districts, a plan calling for interdistrict relief was found to be inappropriate.

Cases from Atlanta, Indianapolis, suburban St. Louis and Louisville are currently in the lower federal courts, and all are seeking interdistrict remedies. The Supreme Court recently summarily affirmed a case from Wilmington, Del. which contained this remedy.

In the aftermath of *Milliken v. Bradley,* the Supreme Court held, in *Milliken v. Bradley II* (1977), that a federal court may order a school board to institute comprehensive programs for reading and communication skills, in-service training, testing, counseling and career guidance as part of a school desegregation plan. The Court found that neither the Tenth nor the Eleventh Amendment prevents federal courts from ordering state officials found responsible for constitutional violations to pay appropriate shares of the costs of implementing the above remedies.

The Supreme Court has recently indicated that it will place limits on remedies for racially discriminatory practices which it considers "excessive." In *Pasadena City Board of Education v. Spangler* (1976), the Court held that a school board that has initially complied with a court desegregation order specifying the proportion of minority students permitted in each of its schools cannot be required to alter attendance zones each year in response to local population changes.

In *U.S. v. Texas Education Agency* (1976), the U.S. Court of Appeals for the Fifth Circuit invoked the traditional doctrine of tort law that a person "intends the natural and forseeable consequences of his actions" to create a presumption that a school district that is segregated in fact is intentionally segregated in finding a provable case of racial discrimination against Mexican-American children. The Supreme Court remanded the case for reconsideration in light of *Washington v. Davis* (1976).

Collection and Dissemination   *Policy #310*
of Racial Information

Title VII of the 1964 Civil Rights Act makes it unlawful on the basis of color for an employer to limit, classify or segregate his or her employees or applicants for employment in any way which would deprive or tend to deprive any individual of employment opportunities or otherwise affect his or her status as an employee. In *Griggs v. Duke Power Co.* (1975) and in *Albemarle Paper Co. v. Moody* (1975), the Supreme Court held unlawful the use of non-validated tests which have a discriminatory impact, and thereby agreed with the EEOC Guidelines, approved as "expressing the will of Congress" which require the collection and maintenance of racial data. Two states, Pennsylvania and New York, have adopted statutes barring the collection of information concerning race on application forms for employment and credit.

Apportionment   *Policy #320*

In a series of decisions the Supreme Court has clarified its one-person, one-vote position as applied to different kinds of political units:

Sailors v. Board of Education (1967) involved a challenge to the procedure used in electing a county school board. The voters in each district elected the members of a local school board. The local board then selected delegates to a meeting at which the county school board was elected. The Supreme Court rejected a challenge to this method of electing the county board, concluding that the county board performed essentially administrative functions. Therefore, it was not necessary that its members be selected in accordance with the one person-one vote principle.

In *Avery v. Midland County* (1968) the Supreme Court struck down a method of selecting members of a county legislative body. The county was divided into four districts, one of which contained 95% of the county's population. The Court declared that units with general governmental power over an entire geographic area may not be apportioned among single member districts of substantially unequal population.

In *Abate v. Mundt* (1971) the Supreme Court reviewed the process utilized to select members of the county legislature in Rockland County, New York. The challenged plan provided for the election of an 18-member legislature from five districts, with each district covering one town in the county. The number of legislators per district was based on the relationship between the population of the district and the population of the smallest town. The need to round off the figures so derived resulted in each district being slightly over or underrepresented. The Supreme Court upheld this plan despite the deviation involved, stressing that the long history of interrelationship between the county and the towns in performing governmental functions justified the slight deviations which were aimed at preserving the integrity of the towns as distinct political subdivisions.

In *Holshouser v. Scott* (1972), the Supreme Court affirmed a lower court decision rejecting a challenge to the method of electing judges to the Superior Court in North Carolina. The process provided for the nomination of judges from separate districts in a primary election, but the final election was on a statewide basis. A three judge federal court concluded that the procedure did not impair the vote of any individual in an unconstitutional manner. The court also rejected the contention that the one person-one vote rule should be applied to the selection of judges, without a showing of invidious discrimination in the selection process.

In *Wells v. Edwards* (1972), the Supreme Court affirmed a second lower court decision involving a challenge to the system of electing state judges. A registered voter who resided in Louisiana brought suit seeking reapportionment of judicial districts from which judges of the Louisiana Supreme Court were elected. A three judge federal district court held that the concept of one person-one vote apportionment does not apply to such judicial districts.

In *United Jewish Organizations of Williamsburg v. Carey* (1977), the Supreme Court upheld as constitutional a New York State reapportionment plan which was challenged by Hasidic Jewish voters as violative of the Fourteenth and Fifteenth Amendments because it increased the size of the non-white majorities in several districts where Hasidic Jews comprise a minority population. It was contended that the plan would substantially dilute the value of the Hasidic franchise solely for the purpose of achieving a racial quota, and that the use of racial considerations in reapportionment planning violates their right to equal protection. The Supreme Court rejected these contentions, stating that compliance with the Voting Rights Act will often necessitate the consideration of race, including specific numerical quotas, as a factor in reapportionment plans. Thus, absent a clear showing that resultant legislative reapportionment is unfairly prejudicial to white or non-white voters, a state's use of racial considerations in drawing district lines in an effort to comply with the Voting Rights Act will be upheld. The Court noted that permissible use of racial criteria is not confined to eliminating the effects of past discriminatory districting.

The Court relied on *Allen v. State Board of Elections* (1969), *City of Richmond v. United States* (1975), and *Beer v. United States* (1976). The *Allen* case held that a change from district to at-large voting for county supervisors had to be submitted for federal approval because such an action could potentially "dilute" minority voting power to elect a candidate of their choice. In *United Jewish Organizations* the Court noted that in the 1970 and 1975 extensions of the Voting Rights Act, Congress was "unmistakenly cognizant" of the dangers of such potential dilution in redistricting plans that separated minority communities among white majority districts. In *City of Richmond v. United States,* the Supreme Court upheld an annexation of city boundaries which proportionally reduced black voting strength in the city from 52% to 42% because the new system created four out of nine wards with substantial black majorities of 64% and thus "fairly recognizes the minority's political potential," and because the annexation was not made for the purpose of denying the role on the basis of race. *Beer v. United States* considered the issue of what criteria a reapportionment must meet under Section 5 of the Voting Rights Act to demonstrate that it does not have the "effect" of denying or abridging the right to vote on account of race. There it was held that the Voting Rights Act would not permit reapportionment that "would lead to a retrogression in the position of racial minorities with respect to their effective exercise of the electoral franchise." In *Beer* this standard was met where reapportionment increased the percentage of districts where racial minorities protected by the Act constituted a majority.

FURTHER INFORMATION
(not policy)

Index to Supreme Court Cases and Federal Law

*We have omitted this date because the suit is currently being litigated.

Name	*Page*

INDEX

(The references in this index are to policy numbers in the *1977 Supplement*, not pages.)